The
CAKE BOOK

BEAUTIFUL SWEET TREATS *for* EVERY CRAVING

REBECCA FIRTH

Author of *The Cookie Book* and founder of DisplacedHousewife

PAGE STREET
PUBLISHING CO.

First published in 2021 by

Page Street Publishing Co.

27 Congress Street, Suite 105

Salem, MA 01970

www.pagestreetpublishing.com

Distributed by Macmillan, sales in Canada by The Canadian Manda Group.

25   24   23   22   21   1   2   3   4   5

ISBN-13: 978-1-64567-344-6

ISBN-10: 1-64567-344-8

Library of Congress Control Number: 2021931361

Cover and book design by Meg Baskis for Page Street Publishing Co.

Photography by Rebecca Firth

Printed and bound in China

To my grandmother, Eleanor Dolores Dimitt Marshall (aka Granny Pete). Your love of sweets taught me the way. You are missed and loved dearly!

My tai tais: Erin, Robin, Louise and Lanelle. You have been my food-loving pengyoumen since our first playdate. I'm so grateful for your friendship. Also, see the Triple Chocolate Threat Cake (page 136) for a reminder of Beijing birthday shenanigans.

And always, Gavin and Stella. I could not love you more!

xoxo

CONTENTS

INTRODUCTION

Friends and cake lovers! I'm so happy *The Cake Book* has made it into your hands! *The Cookie Book* hadn't been out more than a month when I started dreaming about writing this cookbook for you. I wanted to create a collection of cakes that were delicious, accessible and dazzling all at the same time! I wanted to gather all of my favorite cake recipes and mash them up with fun tastes and flavors, so here we are! My hope is that these are the cakes you'll use to celebrate your life and pass on to family and friends for years to come.

Nestled in these pages are quite literally all of my favorite cakes. Pavlovas (pages 146 and 170) for when I'm feeling fancy but don't want to work too hard (read: almost always!). My Birthday Cake (Otherwise Known as the Best Chocolate Cake Ever) (page 16) that I enjoy every year is inspired by the cake my mom made me growing up. And there are heaps of breakfast cakes (page 37) for you to enjoy first thing in the morning—because what could possibly be better than cake for breakfast?!

But before we get started, I have a confession: I'm not a fan of overly decorated cakes. That's not to say I don't admire all of the skill and technique that go into them, because lord knows I do. It often borders on witchcraft what people can do with buttercream and marzipan and fondant. But these aren't the types of cakes that I make at home for my family and friends. I reach for the same recipes that are delicious and beautiful and not too complicated or ornate.

However, to know me is to know how much I love flair. I mean, what's life without jazz hands?! With that in mind, I included simple ways to jazz up your cakes, such as easy piping techniques, sparkling sugar, glossy glazes, delicate flower petals, whipped up buttercreams, a dusting of confectioners' sugar, sprinkles (lots of sprinkles!) and more. Beautiful does not have to mean complicated, I promise.

There were a couple of things that guided my recipe development for *The Cake Book*. I would be lying if I didn't acknowledge that 2020 changed the way I write recipes. I will always be drawn to fun and unexpected flavor combinations, and I'll never shy away from a good baking project. However, when creating these recipes, I aimed to keep the ingredient list as concise as possible without sacrificing flavor. I absolutely adore muscovado sugar, but it's not always easy to find. I tested the Muscovado Banana Bread (page 62) many times, trying to decide if it was worth it for you to go to the trouble of getting yourself some and in the end, it was. I feel the same way about the holiday Muscovado Gingerbread Cake with Salted Caramel Buttercream (page 174)—so get some if you can (otherwise sub in dark brown sugar in a pinch!). I feel the same about the goat's milk needed for the Dark Chocolate Cajeta Cheesecake (page 95)—it is 100 percent worth it. When I include less readily available ingredients (such as muscovado sugar or goat's milk), then a) it's because I really think it's worth it (so try to find it!), and b) I'll list substitutions where possible. Overall, I want this to be as fun and stress-free as possible.

Here are my quick tips for cake perfection:

· Gather all of your ingredients and bring them to room temperature if the recipe requests it (don't skip this step!).

· Make sure you have the correct pan. Going up or down in pan size will change your bake time, so proceed with caution. More on this in The Displaced Kitchen section (page 9).

· Read through the recipe. I have to admit, many times I've just looked at the ingredients and proceeded with how I think it should be done. But you're missing out on all of the great nuggets that the recipe author (me!) has to share with you. Plus, it gives you a good idea of how long it's going to take (1 hour? 4 hours? overnight?) and of any special tools you might need.

· Preheat your oven please! Ovens often aren't warmed to the appropriate temperature even when they say they are. Make sure you give your oven ample time to warm up and come to the proper temperature.

· Carefully weigh or measure your ingredients. The recipes include both volume (cups and spoons) and weight (grams). For accuracy and to get the same exact cake every time, I can't recommend a scale enough. They can be purchased inexpensively, you'll create fewer dirty dishes (YAY!) and you'll consistently get perfect cakes every time. Have I convinced you yet?

· Bake to doneness. Every oven is different; if yours runs hot, check your cakes earlier. If it runs cooler, they may need a little extra time. Look for signs that your cake is done: has it puffed up, gently pulled away from the sides and does the center spring back when gently pressed? These are all clues that your cake is done. Let your cakes properly cool. I get so impatient waiting for any sweet treats to get out of the oven, and I definitely (sometimes . . . often) rush the cool-down time. Don't be like me! Nine times out of ten, your cake will taste better if it's cooled completely. It's one of those crazy things about life that makes zero sense. So set your cakes on a cooling rack, turn them out to finish cooling outside of their pan when noted and then go take a bath, read a book, go for a walk or whatever it takes until that baby has cooled down.

Now go forth and bake some cake, sweet friends!

THE DISPLACED KITCHEN

Here are some quick notes and tips I use in my kitchen to get perfect cakes every time. I could have gone on and on, but we only have so much space! Below are the ones that I really want to highlight for you before getting started.

FLOUR NOTES

The most-used flour in this book is all-purpose flour. I wanted a flour that would consistently produce a fine, soft crumb, as well as be accessible so you don't have to work too hard to satisfy your cake cravings.

If a cake is especially delicate, such as angel food cake (page 22) or chiffon cake (page 32), then I reach for cake flour. A common substitute for cake flour is to measure out 1 cup (135 g) of all-purpose flour, remove 2 tablespoons (18 g) and replace it with 2 tablespoons (16 g) of cornstarch. Sift together several times to make sure they are thoroughly combined.

The all-purpose flour used for recipe testing in this book was unbleached with 11.7 percent protein content. Additionally, I list 1 cup of all-purpose flour as equal to 135 grams. This is a heavier weight than many baking references, but I've found that it's more in line with what an actual cup of flour weighs when people use cups as measurement.

Since nobody wants a dense cake, I highly recommended weighing your ingredients to get the best baked treat, and nowhere is this more important than when measuring flour.

CAKE PAN DETAILS

I can't recommend sturdy, good-quality pans enough. They will help bake your cake evenly, and what can be better than that? When creating the cakes in this book I mostly used NordicWare® pans. Light-colored metal pans are best for baking cakes, but occasionally I'll use ceramic ones when I want to go from the oven to the table (such as with breakfast cakes).

DIFFERENT PAN SIZES

I don't recommend switching up pan sizes from what a recipe recommends because it wasn't tested that way. However, if you do use a different pan than a recipe specifies, you will need to adjust the bake time, so keep an eye on that.

I adore both the angel food and chiffon cakes (pages 22 and 32) in this book (LOVE). I want to emphasize that you do not want a nonstick angel food pan and ideally you want it to have a removable bottom.

WHAT'S THE BEST WAY TO PREPARE MY PANS?

Prepping your pan should be one of your first steps when getting everything ready. I use the moderately vague instruction of "grease your pan" throughout the book. When I use this phrase, it means to either use nonstick cooking or baking spray, or to lightly and thoroughly butter the inside of your cake pan, whichever method you prefer. Baking spray with flour or with "perfect release" on the label is ideal, if that's your method of choice. If I specify a particular method, such as to use butter and then lightly flour your pan, then follow those instructions for best results.

Please note that when you make angel food or chiffon cakes, you will want to use an angel food pan that isn't nonstick and leave it ungreased.

Most recipes will ask you to line your pan with parchment paper. If it's a loaf, square or rectangle pan, I like to cut the parchment so that it covers the bottom and the two longer sides of the pan. Let the excess fall over the sides of the pan, as this will make it easier to lift the finished cake out of the pan. Make sure you press the parchment so that it lays flat against the corners of the pan. When filling the pan with cake batter, I often clip (using clothes pin or chip clips) the parchment to the pan to keep the parchment from moving around. Just don't forget to remove the clips before baking.

To fit parchment to a round cake pan, cut a square of parchment that is several inches larger than the pan. Fold it in half and then fold it in half again. Invert the cake pan and place the closed, pointy end of the parchment in the center of the pan and then cut an arc following the curve of the pan. When you unfold the paper, it should fit snuggly in the bottom of the pan; trim accordingly.

After I place parchment in the greased pan, I often spray it with nonstick to secure it in place.

HOW TO TEST FOR DONENESS

Knowing when your cake is done can be tricky. Cakes may have some or all of the following signs of doneness:

- Slightly domed
- Slightly pulled away from the sides
- Light bronzing across the top and edges
- When gently pressed in the middle, the cake should spring back
- When pressed with a cake tester or toothpick in the center of the cake it should come out with crumbs but not wet cake batter

Since oven temperatures vary (see note above), trust your gut on bake time. If I give a range of bake time and your oven runs hot, check it on the lower end of the range. Conversely, if your oven runs cool it will probably take the longer bake time.

HOW TO STORE YOUR BEAUTIFUL CAKES

We rarely have leftover cake. . . . I'm not sure what this says about us. But in the rare instance that you've found yourself in this unusual predicament, most cakes can handle sitting at room temperature for several days. Once cooled, you can put them back in the pan that they baked in, covered in foil or plastic wrap. Cake pedestals and cake holders are also great for storing cakes. If a cake has meringue or uncooked egg, the fridge would be a wise option.

Humidity will play a role in how long your cake lasts. If it's especially dry, your cake might not be as moist the next day (sometimes I place a ramekin with some water with the cake in a lidded cake pedestal). If it's especially humid, the cake will have a shorter shelf life on the counter. Consider using the fridge, wrapped tightly.

HOW TO EQUALLY DIVIDE CAKES BETWEEN PANS

If you're making a layer cake you want to make sure that the cake layers are as equal in size as possible. There are several ways to do this:

Weigh the batter in the mixing bowl, divide by two and then pour into one of your prepared cake pans until the mixing bowl gets to half of the total weight. Reserve the remaining cake batter for the second cake layer.

If you don't have a scale grab a trusty 1-cup (240-ml) measuring cup and alternate adding one cup to each prepared cake pan. If you only have one pan, add half the cake batter to a bowl and transfer to the cooled, cleaned and freshly prepared pan when ready to bake.

DO I HAVE TO ALTERNATE ADDING THE WET AND DRY INGREDIENTS?

Good question! Too much liquid added to cake batter can make it curdle, and this is a gentler way of adding it to mix. Additionally, adding all of the dry ingredients at once can cause overmixing of the cake batter, which will result in a tougher, denser cake.

MUST THE EGGS BE ADDED ONE AT A TIME?

Similar to above, you run the risk of adding too much liquid at once and causing your batter to curdle. Additionally, eggs add lift to a cake. Mix them too much and your cake might sink in the middle while cooling. Mix them too little and your cake might not have the structure they lend to a cake. I almost always have you add the eggs one at a time, using a low speed on your mixer (if using). Mix until there is no more glossiness from the egg whites on the bottom of the bowl. Make sure to scrape the sides and bottom of the bowl frequently so that the eggs are distributed evenly throughout.

I HATE LEVELING CAKES. HERE'S WHAT I DO . . .

This is more of a confession than anything else. I find it an overly fussy step and one I can't be bothered with. A very important first step toward level cakes is to smooth the cake batter prior to it going in the oven. The cakes in this book should rise relatively evenly so it shouldn't be a problem. If you have a cake layer that rises quite a bit in the middle, you can let it cool upside down, which can help. If it still is too domed, then you should use a sharp knife to cut just enough to even it out.

WHY DID MY CAKE SINK?

Check to make sure your leavening (baking soda/baking powder) is still active. To do this, place a little bit of baking soda in a bowl and mix with some white vinegar or fresh lemon juice; it should fizz and bubble. If it doesn't, discard and replace it with fresh. You can test your baking powder by adding a bit of water to it and it should fizz similarly if still fresh.

Was your butter and sugar creamed enough? Butter and sugar add great flavor (heck yes!), but they also are building structure for your cake. You want the butter to lighten in color and in texture. The butter and sugar should look lighter and fluffier when done.

Did your eggs get over- or under-whipped? Eggs provide structure (among other things) to your cake. Take care to follow the cues in the recipe, such as mixer speed and time, so that they are the perfect consistency before moving on to the next step.

Was the oven hot enough? Ovens are tricky and if yours runs cool then the cake can suffer.

What type of flour are you using? As noted in the Flour Notes section (page 9), these cakes were tested using an unbleached all-purpose flour with 11.7 percent protein. What is the protein percentage of your flour? If it's less, that could be the issue.

Are you measuring or weighing ingredients? If you're measuring ingredients, it's possible that you didn't use enough flour, which would cause the balance of wet and dry ingredients to be off.

HOT TIP! Lastly, if to no avail your cakes are sinking, consider letting your batter sit for 20 to 30 minutes before putting it in the pan and baking. This rest time allows the flour to absorb any excess moisture and results in a puffier cake.

"A party without cake is really just a meeting."

– Julia Child

PARTY **FAVORITES!**
Cakes to Celebrate Life

We all have our arsenal of favorite cakes, don't we? That collection of cakes that we use year after year to celebrate someone's birthday, end a holiday meal, enjoy with friends after a long dinner . . . you get the idea. These cakes are typically decadent, beautiful and almost always to let someone know how much you love them. This chapter is dedicated to these cakes.

One of the shining stars of the chapter is My Birthday Cake (Otherwise Known as the Best Chocolate Cake Ever) (page 16) that is, yes, 100 percent inspired by the birthday cake that my mom made me growing up (and still does to this day!). She tends to make that uber chocolate cake in Bundt form (see page 16 for that!), and I have memories of myself and a friend perched on the counter in a corner of the kitchen finishing up the last bites after the party. In this chapter, I glowed it up a bit into a two-layer, not-too-fussy little number that simply needs some sprinkles and candles. To be honest, I think all of these cakes just need a dash of sprinkles and an inferno of candles to make the mood festive.

In addition to My Birthday Cake, my chocolate-loving friends will also enjoy Bubbie's Flourless Chocolate Cake with Raspberry Whipped Cream (page 28). Bubbie, my cousin Kelly, loves a good gluten-free dessert, and this one I made especially for her (she's my favorite!). The cake comes together easily, and the raspberry whipped cream is the perfect bright and fresh counterpoint to the cake's richness.

Not to be missed is the Super-Simple New Year's Day Chocolate Cake (page 31)! I woke up New Year's morning, and all I wanted was chocolate cake! I wanted something that would be quick, had few ingredients, and was completely unfussy, and DAMN if this doesn't tick all of those boxes and satisfy all of your cravings.

I could easily write a book in my sleep dedicated to my love of chocolate. But I'm always reminded to balance my chocolate love with lots of recipes that are chocolate-free. You can thank my dad for that (he doesn't love chocolate . . . I know, I don't get it either). With that in mind, I created the Angel Food Cake with Blood Orange Curd Whipped Cream (page 22) . . . I mean, can you even? This tastes like a cloud dropped from the heavens. To that end, I cannot recommend the Lemon–Olive Oil Chiffon Cake (page 32) enough; this is one I will never grow tired of.

For those who like a little bit of chocolate (or none) with their sweets, go for the Better Than Boxed Yellow Cake with Whipped Malted Chocolate Ganache (page 19) or the Boozy Strawberry-Basil Cheesecake (page 25)—you won't be disappointed!

MY BIRTHDAY CAKE (OTHERWISE KNOWN AS THE BEST CHOCOLATE CAKE EVER)

My favorite birthday cake growing up was a doctored boxed chocolate cake mix. There, I said it. My mom would bake it up in a Bundt pan, throw some chocolate chips into the batter and I was known to eat half in a sitting. Don't judge me. When we first moved to Beijing, I spent an entire day searching for boxed chocolate cake mix and pudding so I could pass on the tradition for Stella's third birthday. That birthday cake is the inspiration for this gem. This made-from-scratch beauty uses standard ingredients that you probably already have on hand and has a heaping dollop of mayonnaise thrown in to keep things nice and moist. Don't knock it until you've tried it.

MAKES 8 TO 10 SERVINGS

FOR THE CAKE

16 tablespoons (226 g) unsalted butter, room temperature, cut into 16 pieces

2 cups (400 g) granulated sugar

3 large eggs, room temperature

⅔ cup (149 g) mayonnaise (such as Hellmann's® or Best Foods®), room temperature

1 tablespoon (13 g) vanilla paste or real vanilla extract

2 cups (270 g) all-purpose flour

1 cup (85 g) unsweetened Dutch-process cocoa powder, sifted

1 teaspoon (5 g) baking powder

½ teaspoon baking soda

1 teaspoon (6 g) sea salt

1 cup (224 g) hot water

FOR THE BUTTERCREAM

2 cups (340 g) dark chocolate, finely chopped

16 tablespoons (226 g) unsalted butter, room temperature, cut into 16 pieces

3 ounces (85 g) cream cheese, room temperature

1 large egg yolk, room temperature (see note on page 18)

2 cups (240 g) confectioners' sugar, sifted

2 teaspoons (8 g) vanilla paste or real vanilla extract

½ teaspoon sea salt

For the Cake: Preheat your oven to 350°F (177°C) and line two 8-inch (20-cm) round cake pans with parchment paper, greasing the parchment paper as well.

In the bowl of an electric stand mixer fitted with the paddle attachment, add the butter and sugar, and mix on medium speed until light and fluffy, 4 to 5 minutes. With the mixer on low, add in the eggs, one at a time, making sure each is well blended before adding in the next. Scrape the sides and bottom of the bowl to make sure everything is incorporated. Add in the mayonnaise and vanilla and mix for 3 minutes more on medium until light, fluffy and fabulous. Take out of the mixer stand and set aside.

In a medium bowl, whisk together the flour, cocoa powder, baking powder, baking soda and salt until blended completely. Fold the flour mixture into the butter mixture in three batches, mixing each until almost (but not quite) blended. Finally, pour in the hot water and whisk until combined. Scrape the sides and bottom of the bowl to make sure everything is well blended. Evenly divide the batter between the two prepared pans, gently tap on the counter several times to release any trapped air bubbles and smooth the tops. Bake in the center of the oven for 35 to 40 minutes. You'll know the cakes are done when they have pulled away from the sides of the pan and the center is slightly puffed. Transfer to a cooling rack and after 20 minutes, invert the cakes, remove the parchment paper and allow to cool completely.

For the Buttercream: In a medium, heat-safe bowl, add the chocolate and set over a medium saucepan of simmering water. Do not let the bowl touch the water or let the water come to a boil. Stir frequently until barely melted and not quite smooth. Take off of the heat and set on top of a hand towel and stir until all of the lumps are gone. Alternatively, you could place it in a microwave-safe bowl and microwave in 30-second intervals on high, stirring in between until smooth, taking care not to overheat the chocolate. Use either method and set aside, stirring frequently while it cools.

(continued)

NOTE: When using raw egg yolks such as the one egg yolk in the buttercream, make sure you use fresh, pasteurized eggs for your safety. If you have a compromised immune system due to age, pregnancy or illness, then simply omit the egg yolk from the frosting.

In the bowl of an electric stand mixer fitted with the paddle attachment, add the room temperature butter and cream cheese and mix on medium until well combined. Add in the egg yolk, confectioners' sugar, vanilla and salt and run the machine until everything is incorporated, scraping the sides and bottom of the bowl to make sure everything is mixed together. Drizzle in the cooled chocolate and beat on medium until smooth and glossy.

To Assemble: Invert one of the cooled cakes onto a cake plate and cover the top with a thick layer of buttercream. Set the other cake on top, right side up, and cover the top and sides with the remaining buttercream. Finish with sea salt flakes, sprinkles or leave it as is!

BETTER THAN BOXED YELLOW CAKE
WITH WHIPPED MALTED CHOCOLATE GANACHE

Yellow cake gets its warm yellow hue from the ample addition of eggs and butter, two of my favorite baking components. This cake has fewer egg yolks than many yellow cake recipes, but it's just enough to give it that sun-kissed golden hue and richness that you expect from a yellow cake. I topped it with whipped ganache-ish frosting (which is one of my absolute favorite cake frostings). It has four easy ingredients, minimal fuss and whips into the most gorgeous, luxurious frosting you'll want to dive into. The chocolate takes a while to cool and thicken. If you want to frost the cakes as soon as they cool, then prepare the chocolate first, letting it cool while you bake the cakes, and then whip it just prior to frosting.

MAKES 8 TO 10 SERVINGS

FOR THE CAKE

2 cups (400 g) granulated sugar

16 tablespoons (226 g) unsalted butter, room temperature, cut into 16 pieces

2 large eggs, room temperature

2 large egg yolks, room temperature

⅔ cup (149 g) mayonnaise such as Hellmann's® or Best Foods®, room temperature

1 tablespoon (13 g) vanilla paste or real vanilla extract

3 cups (405 g) all-purpose flour

1 teaspoon (5 g) baking powder

½ teaspoon baking soda

1 teaspoon (6 g) sea salt

1 cup (224 g) water, room temperature

For the Cake: Preheat your oven to 350°F (177°C) and line two 8-inch (20-cm) round cake pans with parchment paper, greasing the parchment paper as well.

In the bowl of an electric stand mixer fitted with the paddle attachment, add the sugar and butter, and mix on medium speed until light and fluffy, about 4 to 5 minutes. With the mixer on low add in the eggs and egg yolks, one at a time, making sure each is well blended before adding in the next. Scrape the sides and bottom of the bowl to make sure everything is incorporated. Add in the mayonnaise and vanilla and mix for 3 minutes more on medium until light, fluffy and fabulous. Take out of the mixer stand and set aside.

In a medium bowl, whisk together the flour, baking powder, baking soda and salt and whisk to blend completely. Alternate adding the flour mixture and water into the butter mixture in three batches, mixing each until just blended. Scrape the sides and bottom of the bowl to make sure everything is well blended. Evenly divide the batter between the two prepared pans, gently tap on the counter several times to release any trapped air bubbles and smooth the tops. Bake in the center of the oven for 35 to 40 minutes. You'll know the cakes are done when they have pulled away from the sides of the pan and the center is slightly puffed. Transfer to a cooling rack and after 20 minutes invert the cakes, remove the parchment paper and allow to cool completely.

(continued)

BETTER THAN BOXED YELLOW CAKE
WITH WHIPPED MALTED CHOCOLATE GANACHE (CONT.)

FOR THE WHIPPED MALTED CHOCOLATE GANACHE

2½ cups (425 g) dark chocolate, finely chopped

2½ cups (600 g) heavy whipping cream

8 tablespoons (113 g) unsalted butter, room temperature

½ cup (43 g) chocolate malted milk powder (such as Ovaltine®)

½ teaspoon sea salt

TO GARNISH

1½ cups (191 g) malted milk balls, some whole and some cut in half

For the Whipped Malted Chocolate Ganache: Add the chocolate and cream to a large, heat-safe bowl and set over a medium saucepan of simmering water. Do not let the bowl touch the water or let the water boil. Stir frequently until melted and smooth. Set aside for 1 hour to cool, stirring frequently while it cools until it has the consistency of thick pudding. To expedite, you can also put the ganache in the fridge for 10-minute increments, whisking in between. Repeat this three to six times until the chocolate has thickened.

In the bowl of an electric stand mixer fitted with the paddle attachment mix the butter and malted milk powder until smooth. Make sure that both the butter and the chocolate are a similar temperature before proceeding. Scoop the chocolate into the mixer and mix on medium for about 1 to 2 minutes until the frosting has increased in volume, thickened and lightened in color. Take the bowl out of the stand mixer and with a spatula give the frosting a dozen good stirs to smooth it out.

To Assemble: Place one cake layer upside down on a cake plate and cover with an ample amount of frosting. Place the second layer over the top, right side up, and cover with the remaining frosting. Use an offset spatula or the back of a spoon to make all of the swoops and swirls. Pile the malted milk balls on top of the cake and serve.

ANGEL FOOD CAKE
WITH BLOOD ORANGE CURD WHIPPED CREAM

One bite of this and it makes total sense why it's called angel food. It's light, fluffy, melts in your mouth and is hella easy to make! However, friends, let's talk angel food pans. They are tube pans that aren't nonstick (repeat: not nonstick) that you leave ungreased and unlined. Ideally, your pan will have a removable bottom as well. Angel food cakes are so light and airy that they have to cool upside down so they don't collapse in on themselves while cooling. Some angel food pans have little legs that will keep the cake elevated while it cools so heat and steam doesn't get trapped inside the pan. If your pan doesn't have these little feet, you can perch your pan upside down on top of a wine bottle or any tall, narrow bottle for that matter.

I really simplified my citrus curd recipe for this. My daughter, Stella, thought my old recipe was too fussy so this one's for her! You can also sub in any sweet citrus you'd like (tangerine, cara cara, orange) in place of the blood orange. One final note: if you'd like to garnish with the candied blood oranges, they will need overnight to dry out and be perfect, so plan your baking schedule accordingly.

MAKES 8 TO 10 SERVINGS

FOR THE CAKE

12 large egg whites, room temperature

2 tablespoons (26 g) water, room temperature

1½ teaspoons (5 g) cream of tartar

½ teaspoon sea salt

1¼ cups (250 g) superfine baker's or castor sugar

1 teaspoon (4 g) vanilla paste or real vanilla extract

1 cup (125 g) cake flour, sifted

¼ cup (30 g) confectioners' sugar, sifted

For the Cake: Preheat the oven to 325°F (170°C). Add the egg whites, water, cream of tartar and salt to the bowl of an electric stand mixer fitted with the whisk attachment. Whisk the eggs on medium until they are frothy, 1 to 2 minutes. With the mixer on medium, slowly add the sugar, 1 tablespoon (12 g) at a time. Once all of the sugar is in, add the vanilla and run the mixer for about 1 minute more or until the whisk starts to leave tracks in the meringue. If you swirl the whisk into the meringue and pull it straight up and invert the whisk, the meringue will hold its shape but it won't quite be pointing straight up like stiff peaks. Take the bowl out of the mixer and set aside.

In a medium bowl, whisk together the flour and confectioners' sugar. Gently fold the flour into the meringue, in three batches, until all of the flour is combined, being careful not to deflate the meringue. Spoon the mixture into an ungreased 9-inch (23-cm) tube or angel food pan. Run a knife through the cake batter to remove any air pockets and smooth the top with an offset spatula or the back of a spoon. Bake in the center of the oven for 35 to 40 minutes or until a toothpick inserted into the center comes out clean; the cake should be puffed up and golden. Invert the cake onto a wine bottle to finish cooling completely (upside down), 1 to 2 hours. Once cool, run a knife along the inner and outer edges of the pan and gently coax the cake out of the pan.

(continued)

FOR THE BLOOD ORANGE CURD

⅔ cup (150 g) fresh blood orange juice (5 to 7 blood oranges)

½ cup (100 g) granulated sugar

¼ cup (30 g) confectioners' sugar

2 tablespoons (28 g) fresh lemon juice (about 1 lemon)

1 tablespoon (2 g) blood orange zest (about 1 blood orange)

5 large egg yolks, lightly whisked

7 tablespoons (98 g) unsalted butter, room temperature, cut into 7 pieces

FOR THE BLOOD ORANGE CURD WHIPPED CREAM

1½ cups (360 g) heavy whipping cream, cold

4½ tablespoons (32 g) confectioners' sugar

FOR THE CANDIED BLOOD ORANGE SLICES (OPTIONAL)

1 blood orange, thinly sliced

1 cup (200 g) granulated sugar

1½ cups (336 g) water

For the Blood Orange Curd: Place the blood orange juice in a medium, heavy-bottomed saucepan, bring to a boil and then cook over medium heat until reduced to about ½ cup (112 g) of juice, 5 to 8 minutes. Take off of the heat and whisk in the granulated sugar, confectioners' sugar, lemon juice and blood orange zest until smooth. Add the egg yolks and whisk until completely combined. Place back on the stovetop over medium heat and whisk for 5 to 7 minutes or until it starts to thicken and your whisk feels some resistance. Immediately take off of the heat and slowly whisk in the butter, 1 tablespoon (14 g) at a time, making sure each piece is completely melted before adding in the next. Press the curd through a fine-mesh sieve and into a heat-safe bowl, cover the surface with plastic wrap and place in the fridge for 1 to 2 hours to cool completely before making the Blood Orange Curd Whipped Cream.

For the Blood Orange Curd Whipped Cream: Place the cold, heavy whipping cream in the bowl of an electric stand mixer fitted with the whisk attachment. Whisk on medium until soft peaks form. Sprinkle the confectioners' sugar over the top and whisk until soft peaks return, taking care not to overbeat the cream. Take the bowl out of the mixer and fold in half of the Blood Orange Curd until you still see swirls of it in the whipped cream and it's not completely incorporated. Scoop the whipped cream over the top of the cake. Serve immediately with the remaining blood orange curd on the side.

For the Candied Blood Orange Slices: Fill a large, heavy-bottomed saucepan with the blood orange slices, sugar and water and bring to a boil, then reduce to a low simmer. After 30 minutes, flip the pieces over and cook for 20 minutes more. Set them on a layer of parchment paper to dry out (ideally overnight) before using. When dried, arrange them over the top of the whipped cream and serve.

BOOZY STRAWBERRY-BASIL CHEESECAKE

This classic cheesecake will become your new best friend! We use several techniques that will ensure a smooth top with nary a crack in sight. Also, no precarious water bath! I've been burned by that technique too many times. For an oh-so-smooth and luscious cheesecake: have all of your ingredients at room temperature; mix your ingredients low and slow; press the cheesecake mixture through a fine-mesh sieve to get rid of any lumps or air bubbles prior to baking; and avoid sudden temperature changes. If you follow these Cheesecake Tenets, you shall go forth and bake perfect cheesecake. I updated the traditional gooey strawberries with these fresh and slightly boozy basil strawberries.

MAKES 8 TO 10 SERVINGS

FOR THE CRUST

12 whole graham crackers (6 oz [180 g])

3 tablespoons (42 g) light brown sugar, packed

5 tablespoons (70 g) unsalted butter, melted

FOR THE CHEESECAKE

16 ounces (452 g) cream cheese, room temperature

1 cup (200 g) granulated sugar

3 large eggs, room temperature

1 large egg yolk, room temperature

16 ounces (454 g) sour cream, room temperature

1 tablespoon (14 g) fresh lemon juice

½ teaspoon sea salt

For the Crust: Preheat your oven to 350°F (177°C). Grease a 9-inch (23-cm) nonstick springform pan and line with parchment paper.

Put the graham crackers and brown sugar in a food processor or high-speed blender and pulse until the mixture becomes a very fine crumb. Drizzle the butter on top and pulse until just mixed and it resembles wet sand. Firmly press the mixture evenly into the bottom of the springform. Place the crust in the oven for 10 to 12 minutes or until it starts to turn golden and bronzed around the edges. Set the crust aside to cool completely.

For the Cheesecake: Increase your oven temperature to 400°F (200°C) and place a heat-safe skillet or Dutch oven on the bottom rack (I use a cast-iron skillet for this). Bring 4 cups (1 L) of water to a boil and set aside while you prepare the cheesecake.

In an electric stand mixer fitted with the paddle attachment, mix the cream cheese and sugar on low for about 2 minutes or until smooth and lump free. Frequently use a spatula to scrape down the sides and bottom of the bowl to make sure everything is incorporated. In a small bowl, lightly whisk the eggs and egg yolk and then slowly stream them into the mixer on low. Continue with the mixer on low for 2 minutes or until combined. Add the sour cream, lemon juice and salt, and mix on low for another 2 minutes or until well blended. Use the back of your spatula to smash down any rogue chunks of cream cheese. Press the mixture through a fine-mesh sieve into the cooled crust, smoothing the top with an offset spatula or the back of a spoon.

(continued)

FOR THE BOOZY BASIL STRAWBERRIES

¼ cup (50 g) granulated sugar

¼ cup (56 g) hot water

5 large basil leaves, divided

1 tablespoon (14 g) orange-flavored liqueur, such as Cointreau (optional)

16 ounces (454 g) strawberries, hulled, some halved and some left whole

Place the cheesecake in the center of the oven and pour the hot water into the skillet on the bottom rack and quickly shut the oven door. Bake the cheesecake for 15 minutes and then reduce the temperature to 250°F (121°C) and bake for an additional 40 to 45 minutes. When done, the center will jiggle when gently shaken and the edges will be set. Turn off the oven and let the cheesecake sit in it for 30 minutes, with the door ajar. After 30 minutes take the cheesecake out of the oven. Let it sit at room temperature for about 1 hour. When cool, wrap it tightly in plastic wrap (still in the springform pan) and place it in the fridge to set for at least several hours or, ideally, overnight.

For the Boozy Basil Strawberries: Combine the sugar and hot water, stirring until the sugar dissolves. Add three basil leaves and the liqueur (if using) and set aside to cool completely. Discard the basil if it's darkened. Julienne the remaining basil and toss with the berries and basil simple syrup. Let sit for 15 to 30 minutes or until the berries have softened a bit. Strain the liquid (reserve for a cocktail!) and spoon over the cheesecake just prior to serving. Serve immediately.

> **NOTES:** You can make the simple syrup several days ahead of time. Use more basil if you'd like to amp up the flavor. Omit the booze if you like and feel free to play around with other berries.

BUBBIE'S FLOURLESS CHOCOLATE CAKE
WITH RASPBERRY WHIPPED CREAM

Sweet Jesus, why is this so good, so easy and basically one of life's greatest pleasures? This cake comes together in a snap—no mixer or special equipment needed, and it's a one-bowl wonder. The only hardship involved is letting it cool completely, ideally with an ample amount of fridge time, as this creates an especially fudge-like interior. And don't even get me started on the Raspberry Whipped Cream. This cake is for the chocolate lovers in your life and would be especially fabulous for Valentine's Day.

MAKES 8 TO 10 SERVINGS

FOR THE CAKE

1½ cups (255 g) dark chocolate, finely chopped

10 tablespoons (141 g) unsalted butter, cut into 10 pieces

⅔ cup (133 g) granulated sugar

1 tablespoon (13 g) vanilla paste or real vanilla extract

¾ teaspoon sea salt

½ teaspoon finely ground espresso or coffee

4 large eggs, room temperature

¾ cup (64 g) unsweetened Dutch-process cocoa powder, sifted

1 teaspoon (5 g) baking powder

FOR THE RASPBERRY WHIPPED CREAM

1 cup (240 g) heavy whipping cream, cold

2 tablespoons (14 g) confectioners' sugar

1½ tablespoons (30 g) raspberry jam

TO GARNISH

6 ounces (170 g) fresh raspberries

2 tablespoons (14 g) confectioners' sugar (optional)

For the Cake: Preheat your oven to 375°F (190°C); grease an 8-inch (20-cm) round cake pan and line with parchment paper, greasing the parchment paper as well.

In a large, heat-safe bowl, add the chocolate and butter and set over a medium saucepan of simmering water. Do not let the bowl touch the water or let the water come to a boil. Stir frequently until melted and smooth. Set aside for 2 to 3 minutes, stirring frequently to cool it down a bit. Then whisk in the sugar, vanilla, salt and espresso. Whisk in the eggs until smooth and combined. Sprinkle the cocoa powder and baking powder over the top and whisk into the cake batter until completely incorporated. Pour into the prepared pan, smoothing the top with the back of a spoon. Bake in the center of the oven for 25 to 30 minutes; there will still be some jiggle in the middle. Let cool for 10 minutes on a rack before running a knife along the edge to release from the pan and then invert onto a serving plate (pick something that will fit in your fridge). Let cool completely before placing in the fridge, covered, until serving.

For the Raspberry Whipped Cream: Place the cold, heavy whipping cream in the bowl of an electric stand mixer fitted with the whisk attachment. Whisk on medium until soft peaks form. Sprinkle the sugar over the top and whisk until soft peaks return, taking care not to overbeat the cream. Fold in the raspberry jam until you still see swirls of it in the whipped cream and it's not completely incorporated. Scoop the whipped cream over the top of the chilled cake; I like to leave a border around the edge so you can still see the top of the cake around the edge. Then cover with raspberries and dust with confectioners' sugar, if you're feeling it!

> **NOTES:** This would be so delicious with toasted meringue (page 111) or a thick layer of ganache (page 84) for the ultimate chocolate binge! To make it basic, omit the whipped cream and simply dust with confectioners' sugar or unsweetened cocoa powder. This would also be delicious served with ice cream or crème fraîche.

SUPER-SIMPLE NEW YEAR'S DAY
CHOCOLATE CAKE

I was in the home stretch of writing *The Cake Book,* and I woke up on New Year's Day wanting a super-simple chocolate cake—something that could be ready quickly, with minimal effort, using just a handful of ingredients and one bowl. If you're craving chocolate, this is your girl! The cake is soft, fluffy and moist, and the cream cheese frosting is the perfect contrast of texture and flavor. This is so simple to make and can be served casually with a sprinkle of sea salt flakes, or dressed up with sprinkles for your finest of special occasions.

MAKES 8 TO 10 SERVINGS

FOR THE CAKE

1 cup (200 g) granulated sugar

¾ cup (168 g) good-quality extra-virgin olive oil

2 large eggs, room temperature

1 tablespoon (13 g) vanilla paste or real vanilla extract

½ cup (43 g) unsweetened Dutch-process cocoa powder, sifted

1 teaspoon (5 g) baking powder

1 teaspoon (5 g) baking soda

1 teaspoon (6 g) sea salt

1 cup (135 g) all-purpose flour

½ cup (112 g) hot water

FOR THE SALTED CHOCOLATE BUTTERCREAM

1 cup (170 g) dark chocolate, finely chopped

4 tablespoons (57 g) unsalted butter, room temperature

2 tablespoons (30 g) heavy whipping cream or whole milk, room temperature

2½ cups (300 g) confectioners' sugar, sifted

4 ounces (113 g) cream cheese, room temperature and cut into 8 pieces

2 teaspoons (8 g) vanilla paste or real vanilla extract

½ teaspoon sea salt

TO GARNISH

Sea salt flakes or sprinkles (optional)

For the Cake: Preheat oven to 350°F (177°C). Grease a 9-inch (23-cm) round cake pan and line with parchment paper.

In a large bowl, whisk together the sugar, olive oil, eggs and vanilla until thoroughly combined. Whisk in the cocoa, baking powder, baking soda and salt until blended. Sprinkle the flour over the top and gently fold until just combined. Add the hot water and whisk until combined.

Pour the batter into the prepared pan. Tap on the counter several times to settle the cake batter and release any trapped bubbles. Use a spatula to smooth the top of the cake and bake in the center of the oven for 35 minutes. Let cool on a rack for 20 minutes and then invert onto a cooling rack to cool completely.

For the Salted Chocolate Buttercream: In a large, heat-safe bowl, add the chocolate, butter and cream/milk and set over a medium saucepan of simmering water. Do not let the bowl touch the water or let the water boil. Stir frequently until melted and smooth. Take off of the heat and let cool for 10 minutes, stirring frequently. In a large bowl, mix the confectioners' sugar, cream cheese, vanilla and salt until thoroughly combined (it will be thick). Add in the melted chocolate, stirring until smooth and glossy. Make sure the chocolate and cream cheese mixture are the same temperature before combining. Smear over the top of the inverted cake, sprinkle with sea salt flakes (or sprinkles) and serve.

> **NOTE:** To garnish with chocolate curls (as seen on the cover): In a medium, heat-safe bowl add 1½ cups (255 g) dark chocolate and set over a medium saucepan of simmer water, stirring until melted. Pour over an inverted baking sheet spreading with an offset spatula into a thin layer. Once cool, but still soft, use a bench scraper or spatula to scrape the chocolate gently into curls. Set on parchment paper until ready to use or stash in the fridge/freezer if it's an especially warm day.

LEMON-OLIVE OIL CHIFFON CAKE

I seriously can't believe I almost didn't add this cake to the book! I wrote up the recipe and then I was running behind. But something forced me to make it and DAMN. I know you're not supposed to pick favorites, but . . . This is a very uniquely classic American cake that has Italian vibes with the lemon, olive oil and almond extract. It's so simple to make, you'll be surprised at how fast it comes together and equally surprised at how quickly it bakes up. It's simply dressed in a fresh lemon glaze that makes this cake feel bright and fresh. Serve as is or with some boozy macerated berries (page 54)—YUM! Be sure to use an ungreased tube pan that isn't nonstick.

MAKES 8 TO 10 SERVINGS

FOR THE CAKE

1⅔ cups (208 g) cake flour

1 tablespoon (15 g) baking powder

6 large egg whites, room temperature

1 teaspoon (6 g) sea salt

½ teaspoon cream of tartar

1 cup (200 g) granulated sugar, divided

5 large egg yolks, room temperature

½ cup (112 g) good-quality extra-virgin olive oil

2 teaspoons (8 g) almond extract

⅔ cup (160 g) whole milk, room temperature

FOR THE LEMON GLAZE

1 cup (125 g) confectioners' sugar, sifted

¼ cup (60 g) whole milk

1½ tablespoons (21 g) fresh lemon juice (about 1 lemon)

For the Cake: Preheat your oven to 350°F (177°C). In a small bowl, whisk together your flour and baking powder. Set aside.

In the bowl of an electric stand mixer fitted with the whisk attachment, add the egg whites, salt and cream of tartar. Make sure the bowl and whisk are freshly cleaned and dried. Whisk on medium until the eggs are foamy and frothy, 1 to 2 minutes, and then slowly add in ½ cup (100 g) of granulated sugar. You want it to slowly absorb into the egg whites and build structure. Once the sugar is in, turn the mixer on high until you reach medium peaks; this should take about 1 minute or less. The meringue will look glossy and the peak will slope off to the side rather than stand straight up when you invert the whisk. The meringue should feel smooth when you rub some between your fingers.

In a large bowl, whisk together the egg yolks, remaining ½ cup (100 g) of granulated sugar, oil and almond extract until the mixture is thick and opaque, 3 to 4 minutes. Alternate adding the flour and the milk to the egg yolk mixture in two batches. Then fold the egg whites into the mixture in two batches, being careful not to deflate the egg whites but also make sure there aren't any meringue clumps. Scoop the mixture evenly into a 9-inch (23-cm) ungreased tube pan (ideally with a removable bottom). Run a knife through the cake batter in a zigzag motion to remove any air pockets and smooth the top with an offset spatula or the back of a spoon.

Bake in the center of the oven for 35 to 40 minutes or until puffed up; the top may be cracked and lightly golden, and a toothpick or cake tester inserted into the center of the cake should come out clean. Invert the cake onto a wine bottle (upside down) to finish cooling completely, 1 to 2 hours. Once cool, run a knife along the inner and outer edges of the pan and gently coax the cake out of the pan.

For the Glaze: Whisk the confectioners' sugar, milk and lemon juice until smooth. Pour over the cake, using the back of a spoon or an offset spatula to thin the glaze over the top so all of the pretty nooks and crannies show through. Serve immediately.

CHOCOLATE-ESPRESSO PUDDING CAKE

In my twenties I was obsessed with Nigella Lawson's cookbook *How to Eat*. Her recipe for Gooey Chocolate Puddings was the inspiration for this cake. I wanted a recipe that was a marriage between pudding cakes and a soufflé, would be grand enough to serve to guests and yet would use minimal-ish ingredients. This baby delivers on all fronts. The result is a light-as-air cake that melts in your mouth and is soft and pudding-like toward the middle with a crispy, crackly lid. This is best served in bowls with crème fraîche or classic vanilla ice cream and some good friends.

MAKES 8 TO 10 SERVINGS

FOR THE CHOCOLATE-ESPRESSO GARNISH

2 tablespoons (24 g) granulated sugar

1 tablespoon (5 g) unsweetened Dutch-process cocoa powder

2 teaspoons (4 g) finely ground espresso

FOR THE CAKE

1 tablespoon (5 g) unsweetened Dutch-process cocoa powder

1½ cups (250 g) dark chocolate, finely chopped

16 tablespoons (226 g) unsalted butter, cut into 16 pieces

¼ cup (55 g) fresh-brewed espresso or very strong coffee

1½ cups (300 g) granulated sugar, divided

6 large eggs, room temperature and separated

1 tablespoon (13 g) vanilla paste or real vanilla extract

1 teaspoon (6 g) sea salt

¾ cup (102 g) all-purpose flour

For the Chocolate-Espresso Garnish: In a small bowl, add the granulated sugar, cocoa powder and finely ground espresso and stir to combine. Set aside.

For the Cake: Preheat the oven to 350°F (177°C). Grease a 9 x 13–inch (23 x 33–cm) baking pan and lightly dust the bottom and sides with 1 tablespoon (5 g) of unsweetened cocoa powder, dumping out the excess. Set aside.

In a large, heat-safe bowl, add the chopped chocolate, butter, espresso and ¾ cup (150 g) of granulated sugar and set over a medium saucepan of simmering water. Do not let the bowl touch the water or let the water come to a boil. Stir frequently until almost completely melted. Take off of the heat and stir until smooth and silky. Whisk in the egg yolks, one at a time, making sure each is well blended before adding in the next. Whisk in the vanilla and set aside to cool a bit.

In the bowl of an electric stand mixer fitted with the whisk attachment, add the egg whites and salt. Make sure the bowl and whisk are freshly cleaned and dried. Whisk on medium for several minutes until the eggs are frothy, and then with the mixer on low, slowly add in the remaining ¾ cup (150 g) of granulated sugar. Turn the mixer on high until the meringue is shiny, the whisk is leaving tracks in it and you reach medium peaks. The meringue will look glossy and the tip will slope rather than point straight up when you invert the whisk. It should also feel smooth when you rub some between your fingers.

Fold the flour into the chocolate mixture until just barely combined. Then fold the whipped meringue, in three batches, into the chocolate mixture. You want to make sure that there aren't any chunks of meringue in the batter while also taking care not to overmix the meringue and deflate all of the air you just whipped into it. Pour the cake batter into the prepared baking dish, evenly sprinkle the chocolate-espresso garnish over the top and bake in the center of the oven for 40 minutes or until it has puffed up, the edges have pulled away from the sides and there's still some jiggle when you gently nudge the dish. Set on a cooling rack to cool for at least 45 to 60 minutes before serving. The cake will have collapsed a bit and may have some cracks over the top, which is all fine.

"Too much of anything is bad, but too much Champagne is just right."

—F. Scott Fitzgerald

CAKES TO EAT
WITH CHAMPAGNE
Also Known as Breakfast and Brunch Cakes

Is there a greater joy than eating cake for breakfast?! It instantly elevates any occasion, whether it's a holiday breakfast or just an early Sunday morning. Breakfast cake calls for fashionable pajamas, ditching bathrobes for kaftans and busting out your finest stemware. When we add cake to the breakfast menu, we instantly make our morning casually sophisticated . . . which is how I'd describe myself in my memoir, for anyone taking notes.

When cake is served for breakfast, it often demands (screams for!) dry bubbly champagne. This time-honored pairing is how I got the title for this chapter. Bubbly and cake, my friends, is how you wake up your senses before noon regardless of the time of year, the weather or whatever locale you happen to find yourself in.

In this chapter you'll find my absolute favorite cakes to enjoy for breakfast or brunch, with friends and family or alone on the couch. You'll find a classic coffee cake that's been upgraded with a fresh raspberry quick jam and a heady lid of sweet, crunchy streusel (page 38). This one gets even better on days two and three (if there's any leftover), and who doesn't want to keep the party going? There's also a Glazed Tangerine Donut Cake (page 51) with the crackly, shiny crust of an old-fashioned donut (my fav!).

There are heaps of fruit-based cakes in this chapter. Therefore, I don't want you to feel any pressure whatsoever to trouble yourself with a fruit salad on the side . . . more often than not, coffee cake satisfies your fruit servings as well. If you simply must, macerate some berries with a touch of granulated sugar, a squeeze of citrus and a splash of orange liqueur and you're done.

The recipes in this chapter are adaptable; no need to change out of your slumber finery to run to the market for last-minute ingredients. I will give you substitutions and shortcuts where they'll work and make-ahead tips when prudent. Streusels, jams and yeasty doughs were made for that make-ahead lifestyle we love.

Enjoy and happy day drinking!

RASPBERRY JAM COFFEE CAKE

This is a classic coffee cake but with mega jazz hands added to really dazzle. It has a buttery soft crumb, a bright layer of raspberry jam and is topped with a heady lid of heavenly streusel. Every single bite is a flavor party.

MAKES 12 SERVINGS

FOR THE QUICK JAM

12 ounces (340 g) fresh raspberries

½ cup (100 g) granulated sugar

2 tablespoons (26 g) fresh lemon juice

1 tablespoon (8 g) cornstarch

1 tablespoon (2 g) lemon zest

FOR THE STREUSEL

1¼ cups (169 g) all-purpose flour

¾ cup (165 g) light brown sugar, packed

2 teaspoons (4 g) cinnamon

½ teaspoon nutmeg

¼ teaspoon sea salt

8 tablespoons (113 g) unsalted butter, room temperature and cut into 8 small pieces

3 tablespoons (21 g) chopped almond slices

FOR THE CAKE

10 tablespoons (141 g) unsalted butter, room temperature

1½ cups (300 g) granulated sugar

1 tablespoon (2 g) lemon zest

2 large eggs, room temperature

2 teaspoons (8 g) almond extract

3 cups plus 2 tablespoons (423 g) all-purpose flour

2 teaspoons (10 g) baking powder

1 teaspoon (5 g) baking soda

1 teaspoon (6 g) sea salt

¾ cup (180 g) whole milk, room temperature

¾ cup (180 g) sour cream, room temperature

For the Quick Jam: To a medium, heavy-bottomed saucepan, add the raspberries, sugar, lemon juice, cornstarch and lemon zest and stir to combine. Bring the mixture to a boil, reduce the heat to medium and then simmer until the liquid has thickened and the raspberries have broken down, 3 to 5 minutes. Pour into a heat-safe bowl and set in the fridge or freezer to cool while you finish preparing the cake.

For the Streusel: In a medium bowl, whisk together the flour, brown sugar, cinnamon, nutmeg and sea salt. Using a pastry blender or your hands, work the butter into the mixture until it resembles wet sand and when pinched together holds into clumps. Gently mix in the almonds and place in the fridge. If storing overnight, cover; otherwise, it's fine to refrigerate uncovered for about an hour.

For the Cake: Preheat your oven to 350°F (177°C). Grease a 9 x 13–inch (23 x 33–cm) baking dish and line with parchment paper, letting the excess hang over the sides (you'll use this to pull the cake out of the pan).

In the bowl of an electric stand mixer fitted with the paddle attachment, mix the butter, sugar and lemon zest on medium until light and fluffy, 5 to 6 minutes. You want it pretty fluffy, so if your kitchen is chilly, let the machine run longer. Scrape down the sides and bottom of the bowl to make sure everything is the same consistency. Add in the eggs, one at a time, making sure the first is well blended before adding in the second. Add in the almond extract and run the machine for 1 minute more. Take out of the mixer and set aside.

In a medium bowl, whisk together the flour, baking powder, baking soda and salt. In a large liquid measuring cup, whisk together the milk and sour cream and, alternating with the flour, add to the creamed butter in two batches, mixing each addition until just combined. Scrape the sides and bottom of the bowl to make sure everything is incorporated.

(continued)

NOTES: The jam comes together in about 5 minutes (so easy!); double it if you're feeling especially indulgent, as it's so good to serve on the side. However, if you can't be bothered with homemade jam, substitute about 455 grams (or 1⅓ cups) of your favorite store-bought jam. Lastly, you can make this a classic, OG coffee cake by simply omitting the raspberry jam. This coffee cake is also beautiful with a shower of confectioners' sugar dusted over the top—DO IT!

Add three-fourths of the cake batter to the pan and use the back of a spoon to smooth it; the batter will be thick. Add three-fourths of the raspberry jam and smooth over the top. Spoon the remaining cake batter over the jam. Use an offset spatula or the back of a spoon and try to join the patches of batter together, if possible. The batter won't cover all of the jam; that's fine. Cover with the streusel and drizzle with a couple of spoonfuls of raspberry jam to add some bright pops of color. Reserve remaining jam for serving.

Bake in the center of the oven for 50 to 55 minutes until puffed up and lightly bronzed. The center will be soft but set. Let cool on a cooling rack for at least 50 to 60 minutes and then use the parchment handles to remove it from the pan to finish cooling. If it resists coming out, run a knife around the edge to help it along. Additionally, you can let it cool longer in the pan if you're having a hard time getting it out, as it's a wee bit delicate. Don't stress.

FRESH STRAWBERRY CINNAMON ROLL CAKE
WITH LEMONY GLAZE

This, my friends, is the stuff of dreams. The only thing better than a cinnamon roll is two giant cinnamon rolls stacked on top of each other, stuffed with a fresh strawberry quick jam and smothered in a lemony cream cheese glaze. This is fabulous the day of and equally wonderful the next day. The glaze seems to seal in the moisture of the buns and all of the flavors perfectly meld together. This dough and jam can be made up to 48 hours ahead of time (see notes on page 43!), making this the ultimate, decadent make-ahead breakfast!

MAKES 8 TO 10 SERVINGS

FOR THE DOUGH

1 cup (240 g) whole milk, warmed to 105–110°F (41–43°C)

2¼ teaspoons (7 g) active dry or instant yeast

3¾ cups (506 g) all-purpose flour

2 large eggs, room temperature

6 tablespoons (84 g) unsalted butter, room temperature, cut into 6 pieces

3 tablespoons (36 g) granulated sugar

1½ teaspoons (9 g) sea salt

FOR THE STRAWBERRY QUICK JAM

1½ pints (536 g) fresh strawberries, hulled and finely chopped

1 cup (200 g) granulated sugar

2 tablespoons (30 g) fresh lemon juice (about 1 lemon)

1 tablespoon (8 g) cornstarch

2 teaspoons (4 g) cinnamon

For the Dough: In the bowl of an electric stand mixer fitted with the dough hook attachment, add the warm milk and yeast. Stir well to combine and let sit for about 10 minutes until you see that the yeast is foaming at the top of the liquid. Add in the flour, eggs, butter and sugar, and run the mixer on low until the dough comes together and a ball has formed, about 1 minute. Cover with a damp cloth and let sit for 15 minutes.

Add in the salt and run the mixer on medium for 8 to 10 minutes or until the dough is smooth and elastic. It may be sticking to the bottom of the bowl (that's fine) and slapping the sides (perfect).

Lightly oil a large bowl and place the dough inside, turning once to coat. Cover loosely with a damp towel and set in a warm, draft-free spot (not in direct sunlight) for 90 minutes or until doubled in size.

For the Strawberry Quick Jam: To a medium, heavy-bottomed saucepan, add the strawberries (including any juice that escaped while cutting them), sugar, lemon juice, cornstarch and cinnamon and bring to a boil for 2 minutes. Reduce to a simmer for 5 to 10 minutes or until reduced and thickened. Use the tip of a wooden spoon or potato masher to smash any large chunks of strawberries. Set aside to cool completely before using. I like to throw it in the fridge to accelerate the cooldown process.

To Assemble the Cinnamon Rolls: Grease two 8-inch (20-cm) round cake pans and line with parchment paper. Turn the dough out onto a clean surface. Divide into two, equal-sized hunks of dough. Use a small amount of flour underneath to keep the dough from sticking. The dough will be slightly sticky, but manageable. Add as little flour as possible to keep the dough light and moist.

(continued)

FRESH STRAWBERRY CINNAMON ROLL CAKE
WITH LEMONY GLAZE (CONT.)

FOR THE LEMONY GLAZE

6 ounces (170 g) cream cheese, room temperature

5 tablespoons (84 g) unsalted butter, room temperature

⅓ cup (80 g) heavy whipping cream, room temperature

2 tablespoons (30 g) fresh lemon juice (about 1 lemon)

3½ cups (420 g) confectioners' sugar, sifted

NOTES: This dough can be mixed together, kneaded and stashed in a lightly oiled airtight container in the fridge for up to 2 days. You can use frozen berries for the jam, but you may need to cook it longer to thicken up the jam.

Stretch and roll each hunk of dough into a rectangle about ¼ inch (6 mm) thick (thickness is more important than the size of the rectangle). Cover each piece of dough with a thin layer of strawberry jam; reserve the remaining jam to serve with the cake. Cut six equal-width, long strips from each rectangle (you'll end up with 12 strips of dough total).

Starting with the dough strips from one of the rectangles, roll one strip into a typical cinnamon roll shape and place it in the center of one of the prepared pans. Wrap the subsequent strips around that center roll until you end up with a large cinnamon roll (comprised of 6 dough strips). There should be 1 to 2 inches (2.5 to 5 cm) of space between the cinnamon roll and the edge of the pan. Don't worry about lining up the dough pieces perfectly; it can be a little messy, that's fine. Repeat the same process with the remaining dough strips. Cover the pans loosely with damp towels and set in a warm, draft-free spot (not in direct sunlight) for 90 minutes or until doubled in size.

Preheat your oven to 350°F (177°C) and bake the rolls in the center of the oven for 25 to 30 minutes or until puffed and lightly bronzed. Set on a rack to cool for 15 minutes before taking out of the pans to finish cooling. Gently press down the center of the flattest of the two cinnamon rolls; this will be the roll that's the bottom layer.

For the Lemony Glaze: In the bowl of an electric stand mixer fitted with the paddle attachment, add the cream cheese and butter and beat on medium until they are smooth and cohesive. Scrape the sides and bottom of the bowl to make sure everything is combined. Add in the cream, lemon juice and half of the confectioners' sugar and mix on low until combined. Add in the remaining confectioners' sugar and run the machine on low for several minutes to combine and then turn it up to medium for 2 to 3 minutes or until it's light and fluffy. Scrape the sides and bottom of the bowl one more time to make sure it's fully combined. Set aside.

To Assemble the Cake: Place the flattest cinnamon roll on a cake plate and cover with some cream cheese glaze. Place the second cinnamon roll on top and cover the top and sides with the cream cheese glaze. Serve with the remaining strawberry jam and any leftover cream cheese glaze.

MOCHA LATTE COFFEE CAKE
WITH PECAN STREUSEL

Hey look, a coffee cake with coffee! This one is for the chocolate lovers in the house. It has a delightfully chocolate-y cake base and a healthy dose of espresso (or strong coffee) and cinnamon thrown into the mix to keep things nice and breakfast-brunchy. Streusel loves to be made in advance, plus this cake is just as delicious, if not more so, the next day—which to me is the ultimate sign of a delicious cake! This would be excellent with a morning coffee cocktail . . . Irish coffee anyone?

MAKES 12 SERVINGS

FOR THE PECAN STREUSEL

1¼ cups (169 g) all-purpose flour

¾ cup (165 g) light brown sugar, packed

2 teaspoons (4 g) cinnamon

¼ teaspoon sea salt

10 tablespoons (140 g) unsalted butter, room temperature and cut into 10 small pieces

¼ cup (28 g) raw pecans, finely chopped and toasted

FOR THE CAKE

1½ cups (300 g) granulated sugar

10 tablespoons (140 g) unsalted butter, room temperature

1 tablespoon (6 g) finely ground espresso

1 tablespoon (6 g) cinnamon

2 large eggs, room temperature

¾ cup (180 g) sour cream, room temperature

1 tablespoon (13 g) vanilla paste or real vanilla extract

2¾ cups (372 g) all-purpose flour

⅓ cup (25 g) unsweetened Dutch-process cocoa powder, sifted

2 teaspoons (10 g) baking powder

1 teaspoon (5 g) baking soda

1½ teaspoons (9 g) sea salt

¾ cup (180 g) fresh-brewed espresso or very strong coffee

¾ cup (128 g) dark chocolate chips (plus more to sprinkle on top)

For the Pecan Streusel: In a medium bowl, whisk together the flour, brown sugar, cinnamon and sea salt. Using a pastry blender or your hands, work the butter into the mixture until it resembles wet sand and when pinched together holds into clumps. Toss in the pecans and place in the fridge. If storing overnight, cover; otherwise, it's fine to refrigerate uncovered for an hour.

For the Cake: Preheat your oven to 350°F (177°C). Grease a 9 x 13–inch (23 x 33–cm) baking dish and line with parchment paper, letting the excess hang over the sides (you'll use this to pull the cake out of the pan).

In the bowl of an electric stand mixer fitted with the paddle attachment, mix the sugar, butter, ground espresso and cinnamon on medium until light and fluffy, 4 to 5 minutes. You want it pretty fluffy, so if your kitchen is chilly let the machine run longer. Scrape down the sides and bottom of the bowl to make sure everything is the same consistency. Add in the eggs, one at a time, making sure the first is well blended before adding in the second. Add in the sour cream and vanilla and run the machine for 1 minute more. Take out of the mixer and set aside.

In a medium bowl, whisk together the flour, cocoa powder, baking powder, baking soda and salt and fold into the butter mixture until barely combined. Pour in the hot espresso and stir to combine. Fold in the chocolate chips.

Scoop the batter into the prepared pan, smoothing the top a bit with an offset spatula or the back of a spoon so that it's level. Evenly cover with the streusel and sprinkle with a handful more of chocolate chips (if you want!) and bake in the center of the oven for 50 to 55 minutes until puffed up and lightly golden. The center will be soft but set. Let cool on a cooling rack for at least 50 to 60 minutes and then use the parchment handles to remove it from the pan to finish cooling. If it resists coming out, run a knife around the edge to help it along. Additionally, you can let it cool longer in the pan if you're having a hard time getting it out.

BLUEBERRY MUFFIN SKILLET CAKE

My favorite blueberry muffins are scented with almond extract, lemon zest and loaded with heaps of blueberries—this skillet cake borrows from that same delicious vibe. It bakes up light and moist with bright bursts of warm berries and a crispy top thanks to some granulated sugar that's sprinkled over the top just prior to baking. This is really delicious when served with a drizzle of warm maple syrup over the top. Feel free to use any citrus here—I've made it with both lemon and orange (lime would be delicious as well). In a pinch, this cake can be baked in a 9 x 9-inch (23 x 23–cm) baking dish. Now go forth and eat cake for breakfast!

MAKES 8 TO 10 SERVINGS

FOR THE CAKE

1 cup plus 2 tablespoons (216 g) granulated sugar

¼ cup (8 g) lemon zest (2 to 4 lemons)

¾ cup (175 g) good-quality extra-virgin olive oil

4 tablespoons (56 g) unsalted butter, room temperature

3 large eggs, room temperature

1¼ cups (300 g) whole milk, room temperature

1½ teaspoons (6 g) almond extract

2⅔ cups (360 g) all-purpose flour

1½ teaspoons (7 g) baking powder

1 teaspoon (5 g) baking soda

1 teaspoon (6 g) sea salt

2 cups (248 g) blueberries, fresh or frozen

TO GARNISH

⅓ cup (63 g) granulated sugar

For the Cake: In the bowl of an electric stand mixer fitted with the paddle attachment, add the sugar and lemon zest, and run the mixer on low for 1 minute. Take a big whiff; it smells delicious. With the mixer on low, slowly stream in the olive oil. Add in the butter and mix on medium for 3 minutes or until the mixture is light and aromatic. Add the eggs, one at a time, making sure each is well blended before adding in the next. Scrape the sides and bottom of the bowl to make sure everything is well blended. With the mixer on low, stream in the milk and almond extract and mix for 1 minute more. Again, scrape the sides and bottom of the bowl to make sure everything is well blended. Take out of the stand mixer and set aside.

In a medium bowl, whisk together the flour, baking powder, baking soda and salt. Add to the wet ingredients in two batches, stirring both until just barely combined. Let the batter sit for 30 minutes.

Preheat the oven to 350°F (177°C) and butter a 10-inch (25-cm) cast-iron skillet.

Put half of the batter in the prepared skillet and top with three-fourths of the blueberries. Add the remaining batter over the top, gently smooth the top and evenly sprinkle the top of the cake with the remaining blueberries and ⅓ cup (63 g) of sugar.

Bake for 45 to 50 minutes in the center of the oven or until a toothpick comes out clean; no batter but some crumbs are fine. Let cool for at least 15 to 20 minutes before serving.

BLACKBERRY-LIME BREAKFAST CAKE

You know those days when you're lying in bed and all you want is something sweet with your breakfast (or for breakfast), but you have zero energy for fussing in the kitchen? This is your cake. It comes together faster than it takes to make your Bloody Mary. Immediately put your eggs in warm water and measure out your milk to come to room temperature while you gather and measure out your ingredients and you'll have this beauty out of the oven in less than an hour. Did I mention the tender, moist crumb? Warm blackberries? Bright lime flavors? Or that she's a one-bowl wonder? You're welcome. No really, it's my pleasure.

MAKES 6 TO 8 SERVINGS

FOR THE CAKE

1 cup plus 2 teaspoons (224 g) granulated sugar, divided

2 tablespoons (4 g) lime zest (about 2 limes)

½ teaspoon cinnamon

½ teaspoon nutmeg

2 large eggs, room temperature

¾ cup (168 g) good-quality extra-virgin olive oil

¾ cup (180 g) whole milk, room temperature

1½ teaspoons (7 g) baking powder

½ teaspoon baking soda

1 teaspoon (6 g) sea salt

1½ cups (203 g) all-purpose flour

12 ounces (340 g) fresh blackberries

1 tablespoon (13 g) fresh lime juice

For the Cake: Preheat the oven to 350°F (177°C) and place a rack in the center of the oven. Grease a 9-inch (23-cm) cake round and line with parchment paper, letting the excess hang over the sides (you'll use this to get the cake out of the pan once done). Make sure you press the parchment into the edges of the pan.

In a large bowl, add the 1 cup (200 g) of sugar and lime zest. Using your hands, massage the lime zest into the sugar. Whisk in the cinnamon and nutmeg. Add in the eggs and whisk until the mixture is light and frothy, 2 to 3 minutes. Add in the oil and milk, whisking until fully combined. Sprinkle the baking powder, baking soda and salt over the top and give the mixture a couple of good whisks to evenly distribute it throughout the cake batter. Add the flour and stir until just combined.

Pour into the prepared cake pan and bake for 20 minutes. Take the cake out of the oven and sprinkle the top evenly with the berries, drizzle with the lime juice, sprinkle with the remaining sugar and then place back in the oven to finish baking for 25 minutes. When done, the top will be puffed and lightly bronzed. Let cool in the pan for 20 minutes before using the parchment overhang to lift out of the pan and set on a rack to finish cooling. Serve warm or at room temperature.

GLAZED TANGERINE DONUT CAKE

Ask me how much I love donuts. No really, just ask . . . This has all of the components of your favorite glazed donut, sans the messy oil for frying and, bonus, it feeds a crowd! This cake comes together in under an hour and the glaze helps seal in moisture so it will taste just as fabulous on day two as it did on day one (if you have any left!). Feel free to sub in any citrus: lime, lemon, orange, blood orange, cara cara orange and grapefruit would all be fabulous!

MAKES 8 TO 10 SERVINGS

FOR THE CAKE

10 tablespoons (141 g) unsalted butter, room temperature

1½ cups (300 g) granulated sugar

1 teaspoon (2 g) nutmeg

¼ cup (56 g) sunflower or grapeseed oil

1 large egg, room temperature

2 large egg yolks, room temperature

¾ cup (180 g) sour cream, room temperature

1 tablespoon (13 g) vanilla paste or real vanilla extract

3¼ cups (406 g) cake flour

1 tablespoon (15 g) baking powder

1 teaspoon (5 g) baking soda

1 teaspoon (6 g) sea salt

1 cup (240 g) buttermilk, shaken and at room temperature

FOR THE TANGERINE GLAZE

2½ cups (300 g) confectioners' sugar, sifted

¼ cup (60 g) hot water

3 tablespoons (42 g) fresh tangerine juice (about 1 to 2 tangerines)

2 teaspoons (14 g) light corn syrup

For the Cake: Preheat the oven to 350°F (177°C) and grease and flour a 12-cup (2.8-L) tube pan. Line with parchment paper (see note).

In the bowl of an electric stand mixer fitted with the paddle attachment, add the butter, sugar and nutmeg and mix on medium for 4 to 5 minutes or until light and fluffy. Periodically scrape the sides and bottom of the bowl to make sure everything is well blended. With the mixer on low, stream in the oil and run the machine for 1 to 2 minutes or until fully combined. Add in the egg and mix on medium-low for several minutes. Add in the egg yolks, one at a time, making sure the first is well blended before adding in the second. Add in the sour cream and vanilla and mix for 1 minute on medium until light, fluffy and well blended. Take the bowl out of the mixer and set aside.

In a medium bowl, whisk together the cake flour, baking powder, baking soda and salt. Add to the butter mixture in two batches, alternating with the buttermilk and mixing until just combined. The mixture will be thick and lumpy; that's fine. Scoop into the prepared cake pan, tapping on the counter several times to release any air bubbles and gently smooth the top with the back of a spoon. Bake in the center of the oven for 40 minutes. Let cool on a rack for 10 to 15 minutes. Run a knife along the inner and outer edges of the cake, then place an inverted cooling rack over the pan and gently turn the cake out onto the cooling rack.

For the Tangerine Glaze: In a large bowl, whisk together the confectioners' sugar, hot water, tangerine juice and light corn syrup. Place a rimmed baking sheet underneath the cooling rack and pour the glaze over the top and sides of the cake, just like a donut!

> **NOTE:** To ensure your cake easily comes out of the pan, trace the bottom of the pan on some parchment paper and place inside the pan (ink side down) before putting the cake batter in. If you don't have a tube pan, you could use a similar capacity Bundt pan in a pinch.

"I've always told my children that life is like a layer cake.
You get to put one layer on top of the other, and whether
you frost it or not is up to you."
—Ann Richards

CASUAL **CAKES**
Loaf Cakes, Tea Cakes & Other Shenanigans

Don't even get me started on the joys of tea cakes. Also masquerading as loaf cakes (a most undesirable name), every cake in this chapter can be made in the joy and wonder that is a 9 x 5–inch (23 x 13–cm) loaf pan. You can also use a 12 x 4–inch (30 x 10–cm) tea cake pan, which offers the same capacity plus it cuts your bake time down by about 20 percent (you'll see it in the photos throughout this chapter with the longer, narrow cakes), and it looks hella cute. I highly recommend seeking one out for all of your tea cake needs!

There are so many things to love about these cakes but let's start with the first: at their core, they are dazzling everyday cakes. The banana cake is for once your bananas have become dotted with bronze sugar spots, and the chocolate chip zucchini cake recipe you reach for when your summer garden has descended on you with a squash blitzkrieg.

When I was compiling these recipes, I was really thinking seasonally and asking myself what kind of loaf cakes we wanted to bake in spring, summer, winter and fall. It is my hope that these warm parcels of goodness effortlessly take you through the seasons.

One of my favorite features of this chapter is how the cake glazes, frostings and sugars mix and match between the recipes. The Spiced Gingerbread Cake (page 69) is delicious with the Orange Creamsicle Glaze but would be equally dazzling with a dusting of sparkling sugar or slathered with the frosting from the Ginger-Lime Tea Cake with Crème Fraîche Frosting (page 58). And if you don't want to throw that on your ginger tea cake, it would be perfectly delish dusted in demerara sugar like the Muscovado Banana Bread (page 62).

Most importantly, all these cakes can go without toppings and simply be showered with several tablespoons of granulated sugar pre-bake. Think of this as a sort of choose-your-own-adventure baking experience (the loaf cake edition).

I have several essential tips for you before you embark on loaf cake heaven. First, these cakes need more time to bake and more time to cool as there is more batter in a smaller space. So, don't rush them. Make sure you have a good-quality, sturdy, light-colored, metal loaf pan, as a thinner, darker pan will yield a darker, drier exterior. Lastly, if you have the time, consider letting your cake batter sit for 30 minutes before putting it in the cake tin as this will yield a puffier cake crown (yep, just like a muffin!).

LEMONY HALF POUND CAKE
WITH WHIPPED CREAM & BOOZY BERRIES

This is not your basic pound cake! First, I never want to make two loaf cakes, do you? So here you have just one cake to contend with. A typical pound cake is made up of butter, sugar, eggs and flour of equal proportion. I deviated from this and added some sour cream for moisture and richness, lemon zest for brightness, leavening for added lift, as well as some other flavor and texture enhancers. This cake with some whipped cream and boozy berries is all I need on a warm summer day!

MAKES 8 SERVINGS

FOR THE CAKE

16 tablespoons (226 g) unsalted butter, room temperature

1 cup plus 2 tablespoons (224 g) granulated sugar

2 tablespoons (4 g) lemon zest (about 2 lemons)

4 large eggs, room temperature

⅔ cup (160 g) sour cream, room temperature

⅓ cup (75 g) water, room temperature

1¾ cups (236 g) all-purpose flour

1½ teaspoons (8 g) baking powder

1 teaspoon (6 g) sea salt

FOR THE BOOZY BERRIES

¼ cup (56 g) hot water

¼ cup (50 g) granulated sugar

5 large mint leaves, divided

1 tablespoon (14 g) orange-flavored liqueur, such as Cointreau (optional)

16 ounces (454 g) blackberries, boysenberries and blueberries (or any berry combination)

FOR THE WHIPPED CREAM

2 cups (480 g) heavy whipping cream, cold

5 tablespoons (35 g) confectioners' sugar

For the Cake: Preheat the oven to 350°F (177°C). Grease a 9 x 5–inch (23 x 13–cm) loaf pan and line with parchment paper, letting the excess hang over the sides (you'll use it to pull the loaf out of the pan). In the bowl of an electric stand mixer fitted with the paddle attachment, add the butter, sugar and lemon zest and mix on medium for 4 to 5 minutes or until the mixture is light and fluffy. With the mixer on low, add the eggs, one at a time, making sure that each is well blended before adding in the next. Periodically scrape down the sides and bottom of the bowl to make sure everything is well blended. Take the bowl out of the mixer and set aside. In a large liquid measuring cup, whisk together the sour cream and water; set aside. In a medium bowl whisk together the flour, baking powder and salt. Alternate adding the flour and the sour cream mixtures to the butter, mixing until just combined. Pour into the prepared pan, tapping on the counter to release any trapped air bubbles and smoothing the top with an offset spatula or the back of a spoon. Bake in the center of the oven for 55 to 60 minutes. Let cool for 5 minutes and then use the parchment overhang to take the cake out of the pan to finish cooling on a rack.

For the Boozy Berries: Combine the hot water and sugar, stirring until the sugar dissolves. Add three mint leaves and the liqueur (if using) and set aside to cool completely. Discard the mint if it's darkened. Julienne the remaining mint and toss with the berries and mint simple syrup. Set aside for at least 15 to 30 minutes or until the berries have softened a bit and have started to release their juices.

For the Whipped Cream: Place the cold heavy whipping cream in the bowl of an electric stand mixer fitted with the whisk attachment. Whisk on medium until soft peaks form. Sprinkle the confectioners' sugar over the top and whisk until soft peaks return, taking care not to overbeat the cream.

To Assemble: Place the cake on a serving plate and mound the whipped cream high. Spoon the berries over the top and serve immediately.

NOTE: You can make the boozy berries syrup several days ahead of time and use any leftovers for a yummy cocktail.

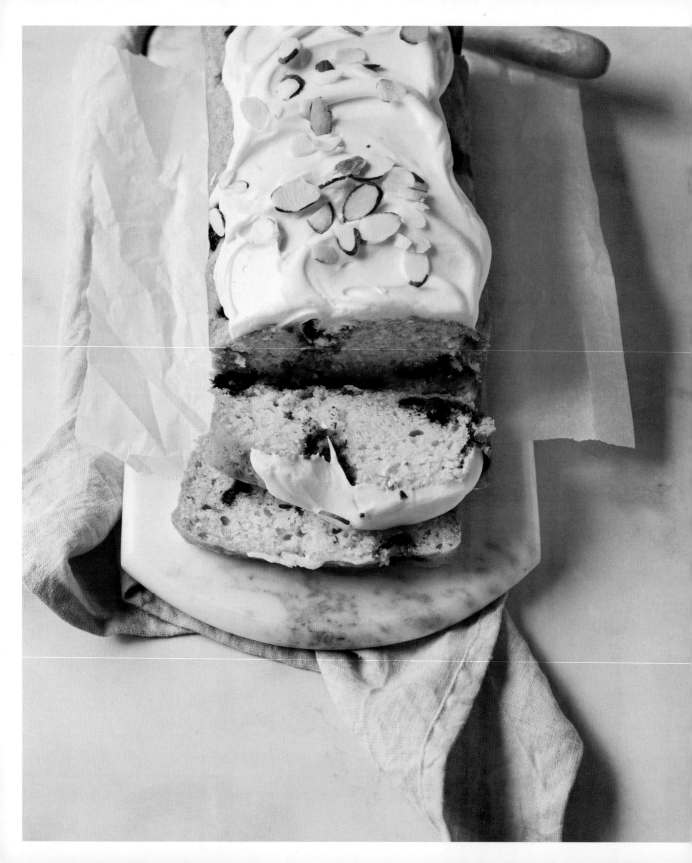

TART CHERRY ALMOND CAKE

I love the combination of cherries and almonds together. We have two cherry trees in our yard, and I'm always looking for ways to use them up. I wanted this one to be easy, zero stress, made from ingredients that you probably already have. This can be made with fresh or frozen cherries. If using frozen, pour half of the batter into the prepared pan and sprinkle with the cherries, add the remaining batter and then cherries. You may need additional time for the cake to thoroughly bake too. When you add frozen fruit this way you don't have to worry about it bleeding and changing the color of the cake batter. The almond soak is optional, but I love a good cake soak to emphasize flavor and ensure a moist cake for several days.

MAKES 8 SERVINGS

FOR THE CHERRIES

1½ cups (246 g) fresh or frozen tart cherries, pitted

1½ tablespoons (18 g) granulated sugar

½ teaspoon cinnamon

FOR THE CAKE

1 cup (200 g) granulated sugar

⅔ cup (149 g) sunflower or grapeseed oil

2 large eggs, room temperature

1 teaspoon (4 g) almond extract

2¼ cups (304 g) all-purpose flour

1 teaspoon (5 g) baking powder

1 teaspoon (5 g) baking soda

1 teaspoon (6 g) sea salt

1 cup (224 g) water, room temperature

FOR THE ALMOND SOAK

¼ cup (56 g) boiling water

¼ cup (50 g) granulated sugar

1 teaspoon (4 g) almond extract

FOR THE GLAZE

1 cup (120 g) confectioners' sugar, sifted

5 tablespoons (75 g) heavy whipping cream

¼ teaspoon almond extract

TO GARNISH

2 tablespoons (14 g) almond slices

For the Cherries: In a medium bowl toss the cherries, sugar and cinnamon to evenly coat. Set aside, periodically stirring. Drain the cherries of any excess liquid before adding to the cake batter.

For the Cake: Preheat the oven to 350°F (177°C). Grease a 9 x 5–inch (23 x 13–cm) loaf pan and line with parchment paper, letting the excess hang over the sides (you'll use these to pull the loaf out of the pan).

In a large bowl, whisk together the sugar, oil, eggs and almond extract until thick and lightened in color, about 2 minutes. In a medium bowl whisk together the flour, baking powder, baking soda and salt. Alternate adding the flour and the water to the sugar mixture in two batches, mixing each until barely combined. Fold in the cherries (if using frozen, follow the instructions in the headnote). Pour into the prepared pan, tapping on the counter several times to release any trapped air bubbles and smoothing the top with an offset spatula or the back of a spoon.

Bake in the center of the oven for 55 to 60 minutes or until puffed up and lightly bronzed. The center should spring back when gently pressed. Let sit for 10 minutes in the pan before using the parchment overhang to lift out of the pan and finishing cooling on a rack.

For the Almond Soak: Whisk together the boiling water and sugar until the sugar has dissolved. Let cool, add the almond extract and set aside. Once both the cake and the soak are cool, place the cake back in the pan and use a pastry brush to brush the soak over the top of the cake, focusing on the sides. If you don't have a pastry brush, slowly pour the soak over the top and give it time to absorb.

For the Glaze: In a small bowl, whisk together the confectioners' sugar, cream and almond extract until you have a very thick glaze. Smear over the cake and sprinkle with the almond slices.

GINGER-LIME TEA CAKE
WITH CRÈME FRAÎCHE FROSTING

Don't be thrown off by the ginger-lime combo here. Let me say firmly: this is a classic citrus tea cake with a touch of flair thrown in to keep things interesting. The lime and ginger are layered, starting with the cake base, then with the ginger-lime soak and, finally, with the ginger-lime crème fraîche. Don't even get me started on how good this is! This cake works beautifully with any citrus, so get frisky. If pressed, you can substitute sour cream for the crème fraîche in a pinch.

MAKES 8 SERVINGS

FOR THE CAKE

¾ cup (150 g) granulated sugar

¼ cup (8 g) lime zest

1 tablespoon (6 g) fresh ginger, finely minced or grated

½ cup (112 g) good-quality extra-virgin olive oil

2 large eggs, room temperature

1 cup (240 g) whole milk, room temperature

1½ teaspoons (8 g) baking powder

1 teaspoon (5 g) baking soda

1 teaspoon (6 g) sea salt

2 cups plus 2 tablespoons (289 g) all-purpose flour

FOR THE GINGER-LIME SOAK

¼ cup (60 g) fresh lime juice

¼ cup (50 g) granulated sugar

1 tablespoon (6 g) fresh ginger, finely minced or grated

FOR THE CRÈME FRAÎCHE FROSTING

2 ounces (60 g) crème fraîche, room temperature

2 ounces (60 g) cream cheese, room temperature

2 tablespoons (28 g) unsalted butter, room temperature

1¾ cups (210 g) confectioners' sugar, sifted

2 tablespoons (30 g) heavy whipping cream

2 tablespoons (4 g) lime zest

For the Cake: Preheat your oven to 350°F (177°C). Grease a 9 x 5–inch (23 x 13–cm) loaf pan and line with parchment paper. Let some excess hang over the sides so that it's easy to get the cake out of the pan when it's done baking.

In a large bowl, add the sugar, lime zest and ginger. Reach in there with your hands and massage the zest and ginger into the sugar to really infuse the ginger-lime flavor into the sugar. Add in the oil and eggs and whisk together until light and frothy, about 3 minutes. Add the milk, baking powder, baking soda and salt and whisk for 1 minute more or until fully incorporated. Stir the flour into the batter and mix until just combined; the mixture will be lumpy, similar to muffin batter. Pour into the prepared pan and tap several times on the counter to release any trapped air bubbles. Bake in the center of the oven for 50 to 60 minutes or until it's puffed and bronzed and a cake tester or toothpick inserted in the center of the cake comes out clean. Let cool in the pan for 10 minutes and then use the parchment overhang to remove the cake from the pan and finish cooling on a rack.

For the Ginger-Lime Soak: Combine the lime juice, sugar and ginger in a small saucepan and stir over medium-low heat until the sugar has completely dissolved. Set aside to cool.

Once cool, place the cake back in the pan. Strain the ginger-lime soak and discard the solids. Brush the soak over the top of the cake. If you don't have a pastry brush, then just slowly pour it all over the top and give it time to absorb into the cake.

For the Crème Fraîche Frosting: In a medium bowl, mix together the crème fraîche, cream cheese and butter until smooth and well combined. Add in the confectioners' sugar, cream and zest and vigorously mix until light, fluffy and smooth. Smear over the top of the cooled cake.

DELISH CHOCOLATE CHIP ZUCCHINI CAKE

This cake is everything you're looking for in a classic zucchini loaf cake: a hefty amount of finely shredded zucchini; a tender, moist crumb; and the most fantastic pairing of mini chocolate chips (an obsession). If you don't have mini chocolate chips, that's fine, use any that you have on hand or omit them completely. I finished off this cake with a sprinkling of more chocolate chips, but it is also absolutely delicious with the cream cheese frosting (page 66) slathered over the top!

MAKES 8 SERVINGS

FOR THE CAKE

2 cups (240 g) zucchini, finely shredded (2 to 3 small zucchinis)

1 cup (200 g) granulated sugar

10 tablespoons (140 g) unsalted butter, room temperature

2 teaspoons (4 g) cinnamon

1 teaspoon (2 g) nutmeg

2 large eggs, room temperature

1 tablespoon (13 g) vanilla paste or real vanilla extract

2⅓ cups (315 g) all-purpose flour

1 teaspoon (5 g) baking powder

1 teaspoon (5 g) baking soda

1 teaspoon (6 g) sea salt

¾ cup (168 g) water, room temperature

¾ cup (128 g) mini chocolate chips

TO GARNISH

¼ cup (43 g) mini chocolate chips

For the Cake: Preheat the oven to 350°F (177°C); grease a 9 x 5–inch (23 x 13–cm) loaf pan and line with parchment paper, letting the excess hang over the long sides of the pan. Place the finely grated zucchini on several layers of towels and press out any excess moisture. Set aside.

In the bowl of an electric stand mixer fitted with the paddle attachment, add the sugar, butter, cinnamon and nutmeg and mix on medium until light and fluffy, 4 to 5 minutes. With the machine on low, add the eggs, one at a time, making sure the first is incorporated before adding in the second. Scrape the sides and bottom of the bowl, add in the vanilla and run the machine for 1 minute more to make sure everything is combined. Take the bowl out of the mixer and set aside.

In a large bowl whisk together the flour, baking powder, baking soda and sea salt. Add the shredded zucchini, tossing to coat. Add the flour mixture to the butter mixture in two batches, alternating with the water and mixing each addition until just combined. When the cake batter is barely mixed and you still see streaks of flour, add the chocolate chips and fold into the batter in as few strokes as possible. Scrape the sides and bottom of the bowl to make sure everything is combined.

Scoop the batter into the prepared pan, tapping the pan several times on the counter to release any trapped air bubbles. Evenly sprinkle the remaining chocolate chips over the top of the cake and bake in the center of the oven for 55 to 65 minutes or until the cake is puffed up and lightly bronzed and a toothpick inserted into the center of the cake comes out with some crumbs and chocolate, but no wet batter. Let cool in the pan on a rack for 30 minutes. Run a butter knife along the edge of the cake to release it from the pan; then use the parchment overhang to lift the cake out of the pan to finish cooling on the rack. This cake tastes delicious warm and even better at room temperature.

MUSCOVADO BANANA BREAD

I absolutely adore the banana bread recipe on DisplacedHousewife.com. It has a fabulous consistency and a great crunch from the sugar crust on top. But I didn't want to carry that recipe over to *The Cake Book*, so I set out to make something thoroughly new and fabulous for you. This banana bread is everything you want in banana bread: mega flavor and tons of moisture, but not much fuss! The muscovado and the demerara are the only non-pantry staples. If you have them (or can get them), awesome! If not, sub in brown sugar (ideally dark, but light will work too) for the muscovado and granulated or sparkling sugar for the demerara. Don't let anything keep you from your banana bread cravings!

One more quick note, I'm about to get controversial . . . but I don't recommend black, mushy bananas for baking. At all. At that point, the taste is off. Pick bananas that have brown spots, but you still see some yellow on the outer skin. They'll be sweetened (hence the sugar spots), easily mashed and still have fabulous flavor.

MAKES 8 SERVINGS

FOR THE CAKE

8 tablespoons (113 g) unsalted butter, room temperature

½ cup (110 g) dark muscovado sugar or dark brown sugar, packed

½ cup (100 g) granulated sugar

1½ tablespoons (19 g) vanilla paste or real vanilla extract

1 teaspoon (2 g) nutmeg

2 large eggs, room temperature

1½ cups (341 g) mashed banana (about 3 medium bananas)

2¼ cups (304 g) all-purpose flour

2 teaspoons (10 g) baking powder

1 teaspoon (5 g) baking soda

1 teaspoon (6 g) sea salt

¾ cup (168 g) water, room temperature

TO GARNISH

2 tablespoons (26 g) demerara sugar

For the Cake: Preheat the oven to 350°F (177°C); grease a 9 x 5–inch (23 x 13–cm) loaf pan and line with parchment paper, letting the excess hang over the long sides of the pan.

In the bowl of an electric stand mixer fitted with the paddle attachment, add the butter, muscovado, granulated sugar, vanilla and nutmeg and run the machine on medium until the mixture is light and fluffy, 4 to 5 minutes. Add in the eggs, one at a time, making sure the first is incorporated before adding in the second; scrape down the sides and bottom of the bowl to make sure everything is well blended. Add in the banana and run the machine on medium for 10 seconds more. Take the bowl out of the mixer and set aside.

In a medium bowl, whisk together the flour, baking powder, baking soda and sea salt. Add the flour mixture to the banana mixture in two batches, alternating with the water. Use a spatula to scrape the sides and bottom of the bowl to make sure everything is fully blended. Pour the cake batter into the prepared pan and smooth the top with an offset spatula or the back of a spoon. Sprinkle the demerara sugar evenly over the top of the cake. Bake in the center of the oven for 60 to 65 minutes or until the top is puffed and may have some cracks. Cool in the pan on a rack for at least 30 minutes. Use the parchment overhang to pull the cake out of the pan to finish cooling. Serve at room temperature.

CARAMEL APPLE CAKE

Is there anything more glorious than apple season? Better yet, caramel apple season? Bonus with this cake: no need to peel apples for this beauty! Use apples that can stand up to baking such as Honeycrisp, Granny Smith or Pink Ladies. The candied apple slices should ideally sit out overnight, so plan your bake schedule accordingly.

MAKES 8 SERVINGS

FOR THE CALVADOS CARAMEL SAUCE

6 tablespoons (85 g) unsalted butter

½ cup (110 g) dark brown sugar, packed

⅓ cup (80 g) heavy whipping cream, room temperature

2 tablespoons (30 g) Calvados (apple brandy)

¼ teaspoon sea salt

FOR THE CAKE

8 tablespoons (113 g) unsalted butter, room temperature

1 cup (200 g) granulated sugar

1 tablespoon (6 g) cinnamon

1 teaspoon (2 g) ground ginger

1 teaspoon (2 g) nutmeg

2 large eggs, room temperature

½ cup (120 g) sour cream, room temperature

⅔ cup (149 g) water, room temperature

2¼ cups (304 g) all-purpose flour

2 teaspoons (10 g) baking powder

1 teaspoon (5 g) baking soda

1 teaspoon (6 g) sea salt

2 cups (250 g) apples, cored and finely diced (about 2 small apples)

For the Calvados Caramel Sauce: Add the butter and brown sugar to a medium, heavy-bottomed saucepan over medium heat and whisk until the sugar dissolves and turns a rich, deep caramel color. Pour in the heavy cream, turn up the heat to medium-high and continue whisking until it reaches a boil, and then reduce the heat to medium for about 5 minutes, or until thickened. Stir in the brandy and sea salt and set aside to cool, whisking frequently. If it starts to separate, whisk it until it's completely blended once again. If not using the same day, place in a lidded container and refrigerate until ready to use. Bring to room temperature before pouring over the cake.

For the Cake: Preheat the oven to 350°F (177°C); grease a 9 x 5–inch (23 x 13–cm) loaf pan and line with parchment paper, letting the excess hang over the long sides of the pan. In the bowl of an electric stand mixer fitted with the paddle attachment, add the butter, sugar, cinnamon, ground ginger and nutmeg. Run the machine on medium-high for 4 to 5 minutes, or until the mixture is light in both color and texture. Add in the eggs, one at a time, making sure the first is well blended before adding in the second. Scrape the sides and bottom of the bowl to make sure everything is thoroughly blended. Take the bowl out of the mixer and set aside.

In a large liquid measuring cup, whisk together the sour cream and water. Set aside. In a medium bowl, whisk together the flour, baking powder, baking soda and sea salt. Alternate adding the flour mixture and the sour cream mixture to the butter mixture in two batches, mixing each addition until just blended. Add the apples and finish mixing, taking care to scrape the sides and bottom of the bowl so that everything is blended; the batter will be thick. Scoop into the prepared pan and bake in the center of the oven for 55 to 65 minutes. The cake is done when a toothpick or cake tester inserted into the center of the cake comes out with some crumbs but no wet batter. Let cool in the pan on a rack for 20 minutes before using the parchment overhang to lift the cake out of the pan to finish cooling directly on the rack. Once the cake is cool, drizzle with the caramel sauce. Serve immediately.

SPICED PUMPKIN CAKE
WITH CREAM CHEESE FROSTING

Does anything say fall more than a pumpkin loaf? This one is generously spiced, has a soft, moist crumb and tastes like a fall party in your mouth. Topped with a super-simple cream cheese glaze, this one will satisfy your autumn cravings ASAP. This is also delicious if you omit the cream cheese frosting and top with mini chocolate chips, a dusting of granulated sugar, spiced cinnamon sugar or some rich chocolate ganache (page 84).

MAKES 8 SERVINGS

FOR THE CAKE

11 tablespoons (154 g) unsalted butter, melted and cooled

1½ cups (300 g) granulated sugar

1 tablespoon (6 g) cinnamon

1 teaspoon (2 g) nutmeg

1 teaspoon (2 g) ground ginger

½ teaspoon cloves

2 large eggs, room temperature

1 cup (183 g) 100% pure pumpkin puree (ideally LIBBY'S® and not pumpkin pie filling)

½ cup (112 g) water, room temperature

1 tablespoon (13 g) vanilla paste or real vanilla extract

2¼ cups (304 g) all-purpose flour

1 teaspoon (5 g) baking soda

1 teaspoon (5 g) baking powder

1 teaspoon (6 g) sea salt

FOR THE CREAM CHEESE FROSTING

3 ounces (103 g) cream cheese, room temperature

1½ tablespoons (21 g) unsalted butter, room temperature

1¾ cup (210 g) confectioners' sugar, sifted

1 teaspoon (4 g) vanilla paste or real vanilla extract

For the Cake: Preheat the oven to 350°F (177°C); grease a 9 x 5–inch (23 x 13–cm) loaf pan and line with parchment paper, letting the excess hang over the long sides of the pan.

In a large bowl, whisk together the cooled melted butter, granulated sugar, cinnamon, nutmeg, ginger and cloves until smooth and well blended. Add in the eggs, one at a time, mixing each completely before adding in the next. Scrape down the sides and bottom of the bowl to make sure everything is well blended. Set aside.

In a large liquid measuring cup, whisk together the pumpkin, water and vanilla. Set aside.

In a medium bowl, whisk together the flour, baking soda, baking powder and sea salt. Alternate adding the flour mixture and the pumpkin-milk mixture to the butter mixture in two batches, stirring each addition until just combined. Use a spatula to scrape the sides and bottom of the bowl one more time. Scoop the cake batter into the prepared pan, gently tap the pan on the counter several times to release any trapped bubbles, smooth the top with the back of a spoon and bake in the center of the oven for 55 to 65 minutes or until puffed and pulled away from the sides of the pan. The top may have cracked, which is perfect. Let cool in the pan on a rack for about 30 minutes before using the parchment overhang to gently pull the loaf out of the pan to finish cooling on the rack.

For the Cream Cheese Frosting: While the cake cools, mix together the cream cheese and butter in a medium bowl until smooth. Add in the confectioners' sugar and vanilla and stir together until smooth and no lumps remain. Smear over the top of the cooled cake and serve with any remaining frosting.

SPICED GINGERBREAD CAKE
WITH ORANGE CREAMSICLE GLAZE

Is there anything more holiday-like than the smell of gingerbread wafting through the house? This little cake has heaps of ginger and molasses to pull out all of those warm and toasty gingerbread flavors. This one-bowl wonder is delicious with either a simple dusting of sparkling sugar or dressed up with the orange creamsicle glaze in the recipe. Queue up the Dean Martin and martinis!

MAKES 8 SERVINGS

FOR THE CAKE

10 tablespoons (141 g) unsalted butter, melted and cooled

¼ cup (56 g) sunflower or grapeseed oil

½ cup (100 g) granulated sugar

1 tablespoon (6 g) fresh ginger, finely minced or grated

1 tablespoon (6 g) ground ginger

1 tablespoon (2 g) orange zest (about 1 orange)

2 teaspoons (4 g) cinnamon

½ teaspoon nutmeg

2 large eggs, room temperature

1 large egg yolk, room temperature

2¼ cups (304 g) all-purpose flour

1 teaspoon (5 g) baking soda

1 teaspoon (5 g) baking powder

1 teaspoon (6 g) sea salt

¾ cup (168 g) hot water

½ cup (170 g) unsulphured molasses (not blackstrap)

FOR THE ORANGE CREAMSICLE GLAZE

1 cup (120 g) confectioners' sugar, sifted

2 tablespoons (30 g) heavy whipping cream

1 tablespoon (13 g) fresh orange juice

½ teaspoon vanilla paste or real vanilla extract

For the Cake: Preheat the oven to 350°F (177°C); grease a 9 x 5–inch (23 x 13–cm) loaf pan and line with parchment paper, letting the excess hang over the long sides of the pan.

In a large bowl, whisk together the cooled melted butter, oil, sugar, fresh ginger, ground ginger, orange zest, cinnamon and nutmeg until smooth and well blended. Add in the eggs and egg yolk, one at a time, making sure each is well blended before adding in the next.

In a medium bowl whisk together the flour, baking soda, baking powder and salt; set aside. In a large liquid measuring cup, whisk together the water and molasses.

Alternate adding the flour and the molasses mixtures to the butter mixture in two batches, mixing each until just combined. Scrape the sides and bottom of the bowl to make sure everything is well blended. Pour into the prepared pan, using the back of a spatula to smooth the top. Tap gently on the counter several times to release any trapped air bubbles and bake in the center of the oven for 45 to 55 minutes or until the top is firm and a toothpick or cake tester inserted into the center of the cake comes out with some crumbs but not wet batter. When done, let cool on a rack for 20 minutes and then use the parchment overhang to lift the cake out of the pan to finish cooling directly on the rack.

For the Orange Creamsicle Glaze: While the cake cools, in a small bowl, whisk together the confectioners' sugar, cream, orange juice and vanilla; the glaze will be thick. Smear over the cooled cake and serve.

MEGA CHOCOLATE CAKE
WITH DARK CHOCOLATE GANACHE

This a quick little number to throw together when your chocolate cravings know no bounds. No need to bring butter to room temperature since we're using olive oil as our fat (this will also yield a hella moist cake). As soon as you decide to make this, put two eggs in a bowl and cover with hot water to quickly warm them up. Turn on your tea kettle so your water for the cake batter is screaming hot.

This cake is infinitely adaptable. Is it the holidays? Chop up some peppermint bark and use it in place of the chocolate chips. Don't feel like ganache? Garnish the cake with chocolate curls (page 31) or sea salt flakes instead. And if you're feeling especially extra (and why not?), smear some marshmallow fluff (page 141) over the cooled cake and then add the layer of ganache. Does life get much better than this?

MAKES 8 SERVINGS

FOR THE CAKE

1 cup (200 g) granulated sugar

½ cup (112 g) good-quality extra-virgin olive oil

2 teaspoons (4 g) finely ground espresso

2 large eggs, room temperature

1 tablespoon (13 g) vanilla paste or real vanilla extract

1⅓ cups (180 g) all-purpose flour

⅔ cup (50 g) unsweetened Dutch-process cocoa powder, sifted

2½ teaspoons (13 g) baking powder

1 teaspoon (5 g) baking soda

1 teaspoon (6 g) sea salt

½ cup (120 g) buttermilk, shaken and room temperature

½ cup (120 g) boiling water

¾ cup (128 g) dark chocolate chips

FOR THE DARK CHOCOLATE GANACHE

¾ cup (128 g) dark chocolate, finely chopped

⅓ cup (80 g) heavy whipping cream

For the Cake: Preheat the oven to 350°F (177°C); grease a 9 x 5–inch loaf (23 x 13–cm) pan and line with parchment paper, letting the excess hang over the long sides of the pan.

In the bowl of an electric stand mixer fitted with the paddle attachment, add the sugar, olive oil and espresso, and run the machine on medium for 1 minute. Add in the eggs, one at a time, making sure the first is incorporated before adding in the second. Scrape the sides and bottom of the bowl to make sure everything is well blended. Add the vanilla and run the machine for 1 minute. Take the bowl out of the mixer and set aside.

In a medium bowl, whisk together the flour, cocoa powder, baking powder, baking soda and salt. Alternate adding the flour mixture and the buttermilk to the olive oil mixture in two batches. Add in the boiling water and mix into the batter in as few strokes as possible, taking care to scrape the sides and bottom of the bowl so that everything is incorporated. Let the batter rest for 10 minutes and then fold in the chocolate chips. Pour the cake batter into the prepared pan and gently tap on the counter several times to release any trapped air bubbles.

Bake in the center of the oven for 45 to 50 minutes or until the center is puffed and a toothpick inserted into the center of the cake comes out with a few crumbs and chocolate but not wet cake batter. Let the cake cool in the pan on a rack for 20 minutes and then use the parchment overhang to lift the cake out of the pan and let it finish cooling on the rack.

For the Dark Chocolate Ganache: While the cake cools, add the chocolate and cream to a large, heat-safe bowl and set over a medium saucepan of simmering water. Do not let the bowl touch the water or let the water boil. Stir the ganache until smooth and silky. Set aside to cool, stirring frequently. When it's cooled but still pourable, pour over the cooled cake and serve.

"That's right. We are single and fabulous."

—Samantha Jones, *Sex and the City*

SINGLE & FABULOUS
Single Layer Cakes in All Their Glory

Behold the single-layer cake, an entertaining wonder that allows you to look fabulous with minimal effort. One layer, easily thrown together and then slathered in something luxurious. What's not to love?

When we think of special occasions, we often think "more" and "complicated" is better. By this I mean a more challenging confection that will keep you up at night wondering if it's going to list to the side or collapse altogether. But, my dear cake lover, I have to agree with Samantha when she says that single is fabulous.

This collection of single-layer beauties uses everything from 9 x 13–inch (23 x 33–cm) rectangular pans to 9-inch (23-cm) round cake pans. They are painless to make from start to finish and can be left simple or adorned with sprinkles, toasted coconut or raw cookie dough bites (YUM).

Stella loves the Strawberry Lemonade Cake with Strawberry Marshmallow Frosting (page 74) that is a sheet cake (named after her!) and loaded with heaps of flavor—perfect for the warm summer months. It can be topped with sprinkles, fresh strawberries or candied lemon peel depending on your mood.

I'm OBSESSED with the Thicc Mint Cookie Cake (page 84) that is inspired by everyone's favorite chocolate-mint cookie (it looks like a giant version of one!).

This chapter has two (TWO) cheesecake recipes: the Big Ass Chocolate Chip Cookie Dough Cheesecake (page 93) and the Dark Chocolate Cajeta Cheesecake (page 95). The former was inspired by the Big Ass Olive Oil Cookies from *The Cookie Book* (LOVE!) and the latter because, well, chocolate. Neither uses a water bath (YAY!) and will turn out silky and crack-free every time!

Go forth, be single, be fabulous.

STELLA'S STRAWBERRY LEMONADE CAKE
WITH STRAWBERRY MARSHMALLOW FROSTING

Bust out the lemons, we're making some cake! Stella wanted a strawberry lemonade cake, so this one's for my baby! This is absolutely loaded with fresh lemons and strawberries at every curve. The cake and soak can be made several days ahead of time, but I have made the frosting the day before, and I think it's best when made the day of serving. The marshmallow frosting on this is barely adapted from my friend and cookbook author Jessie Sheehan. Her original recipe was and always will be an obsession of mine!

MAKES 12 SERVINGS

FOR THE CAKE

1½ cups (300 g) granulated sugar

¼ cup (8 g) lemon zest (4 to 5 lemons)

½ cup (112 g) good-quality extra-virgin olive oil

2 large eggs, room temperature

1 large egg yolk, room temperature

2⅔ cups (360 g) all-purpose flour

1 teaspoon (5 g) baking powder

1 teaspoon (5 g) baking soda

1 teaspoon (6 g) sea salt

1 cup (224 g) water, room temperature

⅔ cup (160 g) sour cream, room temperature

1½ cups (225 g) fresh strawberries, hulled and halved

FOR THE LEMON SOAK

½ cup (104 g) fresh lemon juice (4 to 5 lemons)

¼ cup (50 g) granulated sugar

For the Cake: Preheat the oven to 350°F (177°C). Grease a 9 x 13–inch (23 x 33–cm) baking pan and line with parchment paper, letting the excess hang over the sides (you'll use these to pull the cake out of the pan).

In the bowl of an electric stand mixer fitted with the paddle attachment, add the sugar and lemon zest. Run the machine for 1 minute on low to completely combine the two. If you're feeling it, reach in there with your hands and massage the lemon zest into the sugar to really infuse the lemon flavor. With the mixer on low, slowly stream in the olive oil until it's completely blended with the sugar. Add in the eggs and egg yolk, one at a time, making sure that each is well blended before adding the next. Scrape the sides and the bottom of the bowl to make sure everything is incorporated. Take the bowl out of the mixer and set aside.

In a medium bowl, whisk together the flour, baking powder, baking soda and sea salt. In a large liquid measuring cup whisk together the water and sour cream. Add the flour mixture to the sugar mixture in two batches, alternating with the sour cream. Again, scrape the sides and bottom of the bowl to make sure everything is well incorporated; the batter will be lumpy, similar to muffin batter. Pour the batter into the prepared pan and tap several times on the counter to release any trapped air bubbles. Place the strawberry halves, cut side down, over the top of the cake and bake in the center of the oven for 45 to 50 minutes or until a cake tester or toothpick inserted in the center of the cake comes out clean. Let cool for 20 minutes and then use the parchment overhang to lift out of the pan to finish cooling on a rack.

For the Lemon Soak: In a small saucepan, combine the lemon juice and sugar and stir over medium-low heat until the sugar is completely dissolved. Set aside to cool.

Once the cake and soak are cool, place the cake back in the pan and brush the lemon soak over the top of the cake. If you don't have a pastry brush, just slowly pour it all over the top and give it time to absorb into the cake.

(continued)

FOR THE STRAWBERRY MARSHMALLOW FROSTING

3 large egg whites, room temperature

¾ cup (150 g) granulated sugar

2 tablespoons (42 g) light corn syrup

¼ teaspoon cream of tartar

¼ teaspoon sea salt

½ cup (160 g) strawberry jam

TO GARNISH

Fresh strawberries (optional)

Sprinkles (optional)

For the Strawberry Marshmallow Frosting: To the clean bowl of an electric stand mixer fitted with the whisk attachment, add the egg whites, sugar and corn syrup and nestle it in a saucepan of simmering water over medium-high heat. Do not allow the bottom of the bowl to touch the water. Whisk the egg white mixture until the mixture is thick and frothy, the sugar is melted (rub some between two fingers; if it feels gritty, keep whisking) and it's hot to the touch. This should take about 5 minutes. Ideally you want it to reach 160°F (71°C).

Remove the bowl from the heat, transfer it to the stand mixer fitted with the whisk attachment and add the cream of tartar and salt. Mix on medium-high speed until stiff and glossy and cool to the touch, about 10 minutes (don't rush it). Make sure the meringue is quite stiff and very cool. Take the bowl out of the mixer and fold in the strawberry jam. Smear the frosting over the top of the cake using an offset spatula or the back of a spoon to make swoops and swirls. Top with strawberries, sprinkles or leave as is!

NOTE: For the frosting, you can also use 1 cup (150 g) of fresh strawberries, mashed up, instead of the jam. You can either strain the juice out to use (like Jessie does) or throw the whole lot in there for a frosting that has more texture.

UNA LECHE LEMON-COCONUT CAKE

This beauty is in the vein of a tres leches cake but without all three milks. Traditionally, tres leches cakes have evaporated milk, condensed milk and heavy whipping cream. For this cake, I'm just using coconut milk in the soak, but it borrows from the concept of a heavy milk soak. This cake is loaded with heaps of lemon zest and coconut flakes. You can serve it at room temperature or chilled (how my dad likes it) and it is hella refreshing on a hot summer day. The cake is actually better if it sits overnight in the fridge, making this beauty a make-ahead gem.

MAKES 12 SERVINGS

FOR THE CAKE

2 cups (400 g) granulated sugar

¼ cup (8 g) lemon zest (3 to 4 lemons)

8 tablespoons (113 g) unsalted butter, room temperature

½ cup (112 g) good-quality extra-virgin olive oil

5 large eggs, room temperature

3⅓ cups (417 g) cake flour

2 teaspoons (10 g) baking powder

1 teaspoon (5 g) baking soda

1 teaspoon (6 g) sea salt

1 cup (240 g) buttermilk, shaken and room temperature

1½ cups (75 g) sweetened, finely shredded coconut

FOR THE LEMON-COCONUT SOAK

13.5 ounces (400 g) full-fat unsweetened coconut milk, shaken

¼ cup (56 g) fresh lemon juice (2 to 3 lemons)

For the Cake: Preheat the oven to 350°F (177°C). Grease a 9 x 13–inch (23 x 33–cm) baking pan and line with parchment paper, letting the excess hang over the sides (you'll use these to pull the cake out of the pan).

In the bowl of an electric stand mixer fitted with the paddle attachment, add the sugar and lemon zest and massage the zest into the sugar with your hands. Add the butter and run the mixer on medium for 4 to 5 minutes, or until light in color and texture. With the mixer on medium-low, slowly stream in the olive oil until completely combined. Add in the eggs, one at a time, making sure that each is incorporated before adding the next. Scrape down the sides and bottom of the bowl so that everything is well blended.

In a medium bowl, whisk together the flour, baking powder, baking soda and sea salt. Add to the creamed butter in two batches, alternating with the buttermilk. Take the bowl out of the mixer, add the coconut and fold into the cake batter until just combined. Again, scrape the sides and bottom of the bowl to make sure everything is well incorporated. Pour the batter into the prepared pan and tap several times on the counter to release any trapped air bubbles. Bake in the center of the oven for 45 to 55 minutes or until the edges are lightly bronzed and the center bounces back when gently pressed. This is not the prettiest of cakes fresh from the oven, but don't fret, as it still tastes delicious and will be slathered in fresh whipped cream! Let cool for 20 minutes and then use the parchment overhang to lift out of the pan to finish cooling on a rack.

For the Lemon-Coconut Soak: Add the coconut milk to a small saucepan and stir over medium-low heat until the coconut solids have dissolved. If there aren't any solids skip this step. Combine with the lemon juice and set aside.

Once the cake and soak are cool, place the cake back in the pan and pierce it all over with a fork. Brush the Lemon-Coconut Soak over the top of the cake. If you don't have a pastry brush, then just slowly pour it all over the top and give it time to absorb into the cake. Place in the fridge for at least 2 to 3 hours or, ideally, overnight.

(continued)

FOR THE WHIPPED CREAM

2 cups (480 g) heavy whipping cream, cold

5 tablespoons (35 g) confectioners' sugar

1 teaspoon (5 g) fresh lemon juice

TO GARNISH

1½ cups (75 g) unsweetened coconut, coarsely shredded and toasted

For the Whipped Cream: Place the cold heavy whipping cream in the bowl of an electric stand mixer fitted with the whisk attachment. Whisk on medium until soft peaks form. Sprinkle the confectioners' sugar over the top and whisk until soft peaks return, taking care not to overbeat the cream. Add the lemon juice and give a couple of good stirs to distribute it.

To Assemble: Cover the top of the cake with the whipped cream and create swoops and swirls with an offset spatula or the back of a spoon. Sprinkle with the toasted coconut and serve.

NOTES: To toast the coconut, add it to an ungreased cast-iron skillet and stir over medium-low heat until it takes on a light bronze color. Be careful not to let it burn. Also, feel free to use any citrus in here. For piña colada vibes, add about 1 cup (225 g) of finely chopped (and blotted) pineapple to the cake.

APPLE CINNAMON EVERYDAY CAKE

Lucky for us, apples can be found almost any day of the year, making this the perfect everyday snack when I have an apple cake craving. This was created in the spirit of Marian Burros's plum torte; I love its effortlessness, and I wanted this to have the same vibe. Nine ingredients, one bowl, mixed and out of the oven in about an hour—there is so much to love about this cake. The tender moist crumb, the loads of apple flavor, warm spices and the toasty crunch of the spiced sugar and almond crust. This is the one I want you to drop everything for and bake right now!

MAKES 6 TO 8 SERVINGS

FOR THE CAKE

1 cup (200 g) granulated sugar

3 large eggs, room temperature

⅔ cup (149 g) good-quality extra-virgin olive oil

1 teaspoon (4 g) almond extract

1½ teaspoons (8 g) baking powder

½ teaspoon baking soda

1 teaspoon (6 g) sea salt

1⅔ cups (225 g) all-purpose flour

TO GARNISH

2 medium apples, cored and cut into thin slices (about 388 g)

¼ cup (28 g) sliced almonds

1 tablespoon (14 g) fresh lemon juice

½ teaspoon cinnamon

3 tablespoons (36 g) granulated sugar

For the Cake: Preheat oven to 350°F (177°C). Grease a 9-inch (23-cm) round cake pan and line with parchment paper, greasing the parchment paper as well.

In a large bowl, whisk together the sugar and eggs until thick and frothy, about 2 minutes. Add in the olive oil, almond extract, baking powder, baking soda and salt and whisk for 1 minute more. Add in the flour and mix until just combined. Pour into the prepared baking dish. Starting on the outside of the pan, lay the apple slices one next to the other, slightly overlapping, and work your way to the middle. Sprinkle the almond slices evenly over the top, drizzle the lemon juice and then sprinkle the cinnamon (do this from up high, pinching some between your thumb and index finger). If you find dusting the cake in cinnamon challenging, consider combining it with the sugar first and then sprinkling over the top. Finally, dust the top with sugar and bake in the center of the oven for 40 to 45 minutes or until it's puffed, lightly bronzed and a toothpick inserted into the center comes out with some crumbs but no wet batter. Let cool on a rack for 20 minutes before taking out of the pan to finish cooling on a rack. Serve at room temperature.

NOTES: This is also delicious (and pretty) when dusted with confectioners' sugar. It also pairs very well with some good-quality vanilla bean ice cream. Instead of apple, feel free to swap in peaches, plums, pears or berries.

BROWN BUTTER SNICKERDOODLE CAKE
WITH CINNAMON SPICE FROSTING

What's life without a cookie turned into a cake and stuffed with sugar, spices and basically everything that is right with the world? I love the cinnamon spice coupled with the tang of the cream of tartar. I created that same tang in this cake with the addition of sour cream and buttermilk. This cake is all that you love about a snickerdoodle rolled into a super simple, anytime cake!

MAKES 9 SERVINGS

FOR THE BROWN SUGAR–CINNAMON SWIRL

½ cup (110 g) light brown sugar, packed

2 teaspoons (4 g) cinnamon

FOR THE CAKE

8 tablespoons (113 g) unsalted butter

1½ cups (300 g) granulated sugar

¼ cup (56 g) sunflower or grapeseed oil

2 large eggs, room temperature

1 cup (240 g) buttermilk, shaken and room temperature

½ cup (120 g) sour cream, room temperature

2 teaspoons (8 g) vanilla paste or real vanilla extract

2 teaspoons (10 g) baking powder

1 teaspoon (5 g) baking soda

1 teaspoon (6 g) sea salt

2⅔ cups (360 g) all-purpose flour

FOR THE CINNAMON SPICE FROSTING

12 tablespoons (170 g) unsalted butter, room temperature, cut into 12 pieces

3¾ cups (450 g) confectioners' sugar, sifted

3 tablespoons (45 g) buttermilk, shaken and room temperature

1½ teaspoons (3 g) cinnamon

1 teaspoon white vinegar

1 teaspoon vanilla paste or real vanilla extract

For the Brown Sugar–Cinnamon Swirl: In a small bowl, mix together the brown sugar and cinnamon. Set aside.

For the Cake: Preheat oven to 350°F (177°C). Grease a 9 x 9–inch (23 x 23–cm) cake pan and line with parchment paper, letting the excess fall over the sides.

Place the butter in a small, heavy-bottomed saucepan and melt over medium heat. Once melted, crank up the heat to medium-high. Continue stirring and look for small bronze bits settling on the bottom of the pan, around 3 to 5 minutes. Take it off the heat and pour into a medium, heat-safe bowl to cool a bit.

Once it's cooled a bit, whisk in the sugar and oil until smooth. Add in the eggs and whisk for 2 minutes until thick and frothy. Add in the buttermilk, sour cream, vanilla, baking powder, baking soda and salt and whisk for 2 to 3 minutes more or until everything is well blended. Fold in the flour until just combined and pour half of the cake batter into the prepared pan. Smooth the top a bit and sprinkle the brown sugar–cinnamon swirl evenly over the batter. Cover with the remaining batter, smoothing the top once more and bake for 45 minutes in the center of the oven or until the top is puffed and lightly bronzed and when gently pressed in the center, the cake bounces back. Let cool for 10 minutes in the pan before using the parchment overhang to remove it from the pan and place on a rack to finish cooling.

For the Cinnamon Spice Frosting: In the bowl of an electric stand mixer fitted with the paddle attachment, mix the butter and sugar on medium until smooth. Add in the buttermilk, cinnamon, vinegar and vanilla and continue to mix on medium until smooth, light and fluffy. Frost the cooled cake and if you'd like, dust some more cinnamon over the top of the cake and serve.

> **NOTE:** The vinegar in the frosting can help cut through the sweetness that American buttercreams have, but you won't notice any vinegar flavor.

THICC MINT COOKIE CAKE

Based on America's favorite chocolate-mint cookie, this has a thick, single layer of rich chocolate cake topped with a peppermint cream layer and all glossed up with a rich layer of ganache that seals the whole thing together. This is the easiest cake to make but looks so gorgeous when you cut into it and see the layers. Plus, it's DELICIOUS!

MAKES 8 TO 10 SERVINGS

FOR THE CAKE

1 cup (200 g) granulated sugar

8 tablespoons (113 g) unsalted butter, room temperature, cut into 8 pieces

¼ cup (56 g) good-quality extra-virgin olive oil

2 large eggs, room temperature

1 tablespoon (13 g) vanilla paste or real vanilla extract

1 cup (135 g) all-purpose flour

½ cup (43 g) unsweetened Dutch-process cocoa powder, sifted

1 teaspoon (5 g) baking powder

1 teaspoon (5 g) baking soda

1 teaspoon (6 g) sea salt

½ cup (112 g) hot water

FOR THE GANACHE

2 cups (340 g) dark chocolate, finely chopped

1¼ cups (300 g) heavy whipping cream

½ teaspoon sea salt

2 teaspoons (8 g) vanilla paste or real vanilla extract

FOR THE PEPPERMINT CREAM

8 tablespoons (113 g) unsalted butter, room temperature

½ cup (113 g) vegetable shortening

2 tablespoons (4 g) fresh mint, finely minced

3½ cups (420 g) confectioners' sugar

2 teaspoons (8 g) peppermint extract

3 tablespoons (45 g) whole milk, room temperature

For the Cake: Preheat oven to 350°F (177°C). Grease a 9-inch (23-cm) round cake pan and line with parchment paper.

In the bowl of an electric stand mixer fitted with the paddle attachment, add the sugar and butter and mix on medium speed until light and fluffy, 4 to 5 minutes. With the mixer on low, slowly stream in the oil. Scrape the sides and bottom of the bowl to make sure everything is well blended. With the mixer on low, add in the eggs, one at a time, making sure that each is incorporated before adding in the next. Add in the vanilla and run the machine for 30 seconds more. Take the bowl out of the mixer.

In a medium bowl, add the flour, cocoa powder, baking powder, baking soda and salt and whisk to blend completely. Fold the flour mixture into the butter mixture in three batches, mixing each until almost (but not quite) blended. Finally, pour in the hot water and whisk to combine. Scrape the sides and bottom of the bowl to make sure everything is well blended. Pour into the prepared baking dish. Tap on the counter several times to settle the cake batter and release any trapped bubbles. Use a spatula to smooth and even out the top of the cake and bake in the center of the oven for 35 to 40 minutes. Let cool on a rack for 20 minutes and then turn out of the pan to finish cooling.

For the Ganache: In a large, heat-safe bowl, add the chocolate, cream and sea salt; set over a medium saucepan of simmering water. Do not let the bowl touch the water or let the water boil. Stir frequently until melted and smooth and then stir in the vanilla. Let the ganache sit, stirring frequently, until cool to the touch but still fluid.

For the Peppermint Cream: Place the butter, shortening and mint in the bowl of an electric stand mixer fitted with the paddle attachment. Mix on medium-low until well blended. Add in the confectioners' sugar, peppermint extract and milk and continue blending until whipped, smooth and creamy.

To Assemble: Smear the peppermint cream evenly over the top of the cooled cake, making it as smooth as possible. Try to make the edges sharp angles that follow the line of the cake. Set in the fridge for 30 minutes. Place a cooling rack over a rimmed baking sheet and set the cake on top. Pour the ganache evenly over the cake using an offset spatula or the back of a spoon to smooth it and make sure the entire cake is evenly covered. Return to the fridge to set for at least 30 minutes and serve.

GRANNY PETE'S CHOCOLATE CAKE
WITH MARSHMALLOW FROSTING

I only included two recipes from DisplacedHousewife.com, and I knew this had to be one of them! Not only did I create this cake in honor of my grandmother, Granny Pete, who happened to love sweets and chocolate as much as I do, but it is just a really fabulous, go-to, "let's flipping celebrate life" chocolate cake! It honestly tastes like an enormous, deconstructed Ding Dong, which I was mildly addicted to in high school. If you loved Ding Dongs and are obsessed with chocolate and marshmallow frosting, this easy, delicious cake has your name written all over it!

MAKES 12 SERVINGS

FOR THE CAKE

16 tablespoons (226 g) unsalted butter, room temperature, cut into 16 pieces

2 cups (400 g) granulated sugar

2–3 teaspoons (4–6 g) finely ground espresso

½ cup (120 g) whole milk, room temperature

⅔ cup (160 g) sour cream, room temperature

3 large eggs, room temperature

1 tablespoon (13 g) vanilla paste or real vanilla extract

2 cups (270 g) all-purpose flour

1 cup (85 g) unsweetened Dutch-process cocoa powder, sifted

1 teaspoon (5 g) baking powder

1 teaspoon (5 g) baking soda

1 teaspoon (6 g) sea salt

½ cup (112 g) hot, fresh-brewed espresso or strong coffee

For the Cake: Preheat oven to 350°F (177°C). In the bowl of an electric stand mixer fitted with the paddle attachment, add the butter, sugar and finely ground espresso and mix on medium speed until light and fluffy, 4 to 5 minutes. With the mixer on low, stream in the milk. Scrape the sides and bottom of the bowl to make sure everything is well blended. Add in the sour cream and mix for 1 minute more until light, fluffy and fabulous. With the mixer on low, add in the eggs, one at a time, making sure that each is well blended before adding in the next. Add in the vanilla and run the machine for 30 seconds more. Take the bowl out of the mixer.

In a medium bowl, whisk together the flour, cocoa powder, baking powder, baking soda and salt. Fold the flour mixture into the butter mixture in three batches, mixing each until almost (but not quite) blended. Finally, pour in the hot espresso and stir. Scrape the sides and bottom of the bowl to make sure everything is well blended. Stir the batter enough that everything is combined but being cautious not to mix too much as we don't want a tough cake. Set aside.

Grease your 9 x 13–inch (23 x 33–cm) baking dish and line with parchment paper, taking care that it lays flat against the dish, letting the excess hang over the sides of the pan (you'll use these to pull the cake out of the pan). Pour the batter into the prepared baking dish. Tap on the counter several times to settle the cake batter and release any trapped bubbles. Use a spatula to smooth and even out the top of the cake batter. Bake in the center of the oven for 40 to 43 minutes. Use a toothpick or cake tester to test for doneness. Some moisture and crumbs are fine, but if it's coated in cake batter, bake it for several minutes more. Another way to test for doneness: press the center part of the cake gently, and it should spring back when your finger lifts.

(continued)

GRANNY PETE'S CHOCOLATE CAKE
WITH MARSHMALLOW FROSTING (CONT.)

FOR THE ESPRESSO SOAK

½ cup (112 g) fresh-brewed espresso or strong coffee

¼ cup (50 g) granulated sugar

FOR THE MARSHMALLOW FROSTING

3 large egg whites

¾ cup (150 g) granulated sugar

2 tablespoons (42 g) light corn syrup

¼ teaspoon cream of tartar

¼ teaspoon sea salt

½ teaspoon vanilla paste or real vanilla extract

FOR GARNISH

Sprinkles (optional)

For the Espresso Soak: Combine the espresso and sugar in a small saucepan and stir over medium-low heat until the sugar has completely dissolved. Set aside to cool a bit.

Let the cake sit for 10 minutes and then brush the Espresso Soak over the top of the cake. If you don't have a pastry brush, then just slowly pour it all over the top, giving it time to absorb into the cake. After another 20 minutes, use the parchment overhang to lift the cake out of the baking dish and finish cooling completely on a cooling rack.

For the Marshmallow Frosting: Add the egg whites, sugar and corn syrup in the clean bowl of an electric stand mixer and nestle it in a saucepan of simmering water over medium-high heat. Do not allow the bottom of the bowl to touch the water. Whisk until the mixture is opaque and frothy, the sugar is melted (rub some between two fingers; if it feels gritty, keep whisking) and it's warm to the touch. Remove the bowl from the heat and transfer it to the stand mixer fitted with the whisk attachment. Add the cream of tartar and salt and mix on medium-high speed until stiff and glossy and cool to the touch, 3 to 5 minutes. Add in the vanilla and run the machine for 30 seconds more or until combined. Smear over the top of the cooled cake. Sprinkle with sprinkles, if you're feeling it.

CHOCOLATE-PEANUT BUTTER
GRAHAM CRACKER CAKE

My sister, Katy, had graham crackers with peanut butter during a hospital stay and couldn't stop talking about how yummy it was and how it would make a good cake. I totally agreed and loved the idea of peanut butter, graham crackers and chocolate all mashed together into cake form. This is a super light, moist chocolate cake with the added cinnamon-sweetness of graham crackers lingering in the background. The peanut butter frosting is luxurious . . . there's no other way to describe it.

MAKES 10 TO 12 SERVINGS

FOR THE CAKE

16 tablespoons (226 g) unsalted butter, room temperature, cut into 16 pieces

1 cup (200 g) granulated sugar

1 cup (220 g) light brown sugar, packed

2 teaspoons (4 g) cinnamon

3 large eggs, room temperature

1 cup (240 g) sour cream, room temperature

1 tablespoon (13 g) vanilla paste or real vanilla extract

1¾ cups (237 g) all-purpose flour

1 cup (85 g) unsweetened Dutch-process cocoa powder, sifted

¼ cup (41 g) finely ground graham crackers (about 2½ whole graham crackers)

2 teaspoons (10 g) baking powder

1 teaspoon (5 g) baking soda

1 teaspoon (6 g) sea salt

¾ cup (168 g) hot water

For the Cake: Preheat the oven to 350°F (177°C). Grease a 9 x 13–inch (23 x 33–cm) baking pan and line with parchment paper, letting the excess hang over the sides. Set aside.

In the bowl of an electric stand mixer fitted with the paddle attachment, add the butter, granulated sugar, brown sugar and cinnamon and mix on medium speed until light and fluffy, 4 to 5 minutes. With the mixer on low, add in the eggs, one at a time, making sure that each is well blended before adding in the next. Scrape the sides and bottom of the bowl to make sure everything is well blended. Add in the sour cream and vanilla and mix for 1 minute more until light, fluffy and fabulous. Take the bowl out of the mixer and set aside.

In a medium bowl, whisk together the flour, cocoa powder, finely ground graham crackers, baking powder, baking soda and salt and whisk to blend completely. Fold the flour mixture into the butter mixture in two batches, mixing each until almost (but not quite) blended. Finally, pour in the hot water and whisk to combine. Scrape the sides and bottom of the bowl to make sure everything is well blended. This batter is lumpy, so take care not to overmix. Pour the batter into the prepared baking dish. Tap on the counter several times to settle the cake batter and release any trapped bubbles. Use a spatula to smooth and even out the top of the cake and bake in the center of the oven for 45 to 50 minutes.

Let cool on a rack for 20 minutes and then use the parchment overhang to lift the cake out of the baking dish and finish cooling completely on a cooling rack.

(continued)

CHOCOLATE-PEANUT BUTTER
GRAHAM CRACKER CAKE (CONT.)

**FOR THE PEANUT BUTTER
BUTTERCREAM**

1 cup (340 g) smooth peanut butter

16 tablespoons (226 g) unsalted
butter, room temperature, cut into
16 pieces

2 cups (240 g) confectioners' sugar,
sifted

1 large egg yolk, room temperature
(optional)

2 tablespoons (30 g) whole milk,
room temperature

1 tablespoon (13 g) vanilla paste or
real vanilla extract

1 teaspoon (6 g) sea salt

For the Peanut Butter Buttercream: In the bowl of an electric stand mixer
fitted with the paddle attachment, add the peanut butter and butter and run
on medium until well combined. Add in the confectioners' sugar, egg yolk (if
using), milk, vanilla and salt and run until everything is incorporated; scrape the
sides and bottom of the bowl to make sure everything is mixed together. Smear
the buttercream over the cooled cake; I like to leave a 1-inch (2.5-cm) border
free from buttercream so you can see the cake.

NOTES: In a pinch, you can make this a classic chocolate-peanut
butter cake by omitting the graham crackers in the cake and replacing
it 1:1 with more all-purpose flour. The yolk in the buttercream gives it
a silky, luscious texture. If using, make sure your egg is pasteurized.
Feel free to omit if you're not feeling it and the buttercream will still
be delish. If you use the raw egg, refrigerate any cake leftovers!

BIG ASS CHOCOLATE CHIP
COOKIE DOUGH CHEESECAKE

What's not to love?! This cheesecake is flavored with brown sugar and vanilla a̶
cookie dough bites sitting atop a thick, chocolate-graham crust. It is covered in
finished with my favorite no-egg cookie dough bites (these are good in ice crea̶
even just to snack on!). The cheesecake should have at least overnight in the frid̶
eating accordingly!

MAKES 8 TO 10 SERVINGS

FOR THE COOKIE DOUGH BALLS

9 tablespoons (127 g) unsalted butter

½ cup (110 g) dark brown sugar, packed

¼ cup (50 g) granulated sugar

2 tablespoons (30 g) whole milk, room temperature

1 tablespoon (13 g) vanilla paste or real vanilla extract

½ teaspoon sea salt

1¾ cups (237 g) all-purpose flour

¾ cup (128 g) mini chocolate chips

FOR THE CRUST

16 whole graham crackers (9 oz [249 g])

¼ cup (55 g) light brown sugar, packed

3 tablespoons (18 g) unsweetened Dutch-process cocoa powder, sifted

½ teaspoon sea salt

8 tablespoons (113 g) unsalted butter, melted

For the Cookie Dough Balls: Place the̶
saucepan and melt over medium heat. O̶ ̶ ̶ ̶eat to
medium-high. Continue stirring and look ̶ ̶ ̶ ̶ bits that will start to
settle on the bottom of the pan. It will smell deliciously nutty and caramel-y.
This should take 3 to 5 minutes. Once this happens, take it off the heat and
pour into a large, heat-safe bowl to cool. Once cool, add in the brown sugar,
granulated sugar, milk, vanilla and sea salt, stirring to completely combine. Stir
in the flour and chocolate chips until just combined. Roll 1-teaspoon (5-g)-
sized balls and place them in a lidded container, separating the layers with
parchment paper, and stash in the fridge until ready to use. The dough can be a
little crumbly, so lightly dampen your hands to help with shaping if it resists
rolling into balls.

For the Crust: Preheat your oven to 350°F (177°C). Grease a 9-inch (23-cm)
nonstick springform pan and line with parchment paper.

Put the graham crackers and brown sugar in a food processor or high-speed
blender and pulse until the mixture becomes a very fine crumb. Add in the
cocoa powder and sea salt and pulse to combine. Drizzle the butter on top and
pulse until just mixed and it resembles wet sand. Firmly press the mixture
evenly into the bottom of the springform. Place the crust in the oven for 10 to
12 minutes or until it starts to turn golden and bronzed around the edges. Set
the crust aside to cool completely.

(continued)

...SECAKE

...2 g) cream cheese,
...perature

...(220 g) light brown sugar,
...cked

3 large eggs, room temperature

1 large egg yolk, room temperature

16 ounces (454 g) sour cream, room temperature

1½ tablespoons (19 g) vanilla paste or real vanilla extract

½ teaspoon sea salt

FOR THE GANACHE

1¼ cups (213 g) dark chocolate, finely chopped

1 cup (240 g) heavy whipping cream

½ teaspoon sea salt

2 teaspoons (8 g) vanilla paste or real vanilla extract

NOTES: The cookie dough bites contain raw, uncooked flour, which can pose safety concerns. To quickly kill any bacteria, place the flour in a microwave-safe bowl and cook for 1 minute, stirring midway through, or until it reaches 165°F (74°C) on an instant-read thermometer.

For the photos, I reserved some of the ganache to dip half of the remaining cookie dough balls; allow time for the dipped dough balls to set in the fridge before using.

For the Cheesecake: Increase the oven temperature to 400°F (200°C) and place a heat-safe skillet or Dutch oven on the lowest rack. Bring 4 cups (1 L) of water to a boil and set aside while you prepare the cheesecake.

In the bowl of an electric stand mixer fitted with the paddle attachment, mix the cream cheese and sugar on low for about 2 minutes or until smooth and lump free. Frequently use a spatula to scrape down the sides and bottom of the bowl to make sure everything is incorporated.

In a small bowl, lightly whisk the eggs and egg yolk and then slowly stream them into the bowl with the mixer on low. Continue with the mixer on low for 2 minutes or until combined. Add the sour cream, vanilla and salt and mix on low for another 2 minutes or until well blended. Use the back of your spatula to smash down any rogue chunks of cream cheese. Press the mixture through a sieve into a clean bowl.

Place half of the cookie dough balls on the crust and pour the cheesecake filling over them, smoothing the top with an offset spatula or the back of a spoon. Place the cheesecake in the center of the oven and pour the hot water into the skillet on the bottom rack and quickly shut the oven door. Bake the cheesecake for 15 minutes and then reduce the oven to 250°F (121°C) and bake for an additional 40 to 45 minutes. When done, the center will jiggle when gently shaken and the edges will be set. Turn off the oven and let the cheesecake sit in the oven for 30 minutes, with the door open. After 30 minutes, take the cheesecake out of the oven. Let it sit at room temperature for about 1 hour. When cool, wrap tightly in plastic wrap (still in the springform pan) and place in the fridge to set overnight.

For the Ganache: In a large, heat-safe bowl add the chocolate, cream and sea salt and set over a medium saucepan of simmering water. Do not let the bowl touch the water or let the water boil. Stir frequently until melted and smooth. Take off of the heat and whisk in the vanilla. Set aside for 1 to 2 hours to cool, stirring frequently until it has cooled but is still pourable. Take the removable edge off of the cheesecake and set it on a cooling rack with a rimmed baking sheet beneath it. Pour the ganache over the cheesecake using an offset spatula or the back of a spoon to smooth the top and make sure everything is evenly covered. Set back in the fridge until ready to serve. Cover with the remaining dough balls just prior to serving.

DARK CHOCOLATE CAJETA CHEESECAKE

This is the most divine chocolate cheesecake. It features a smooth, silky, rich chocolate filling, crispy chocolate graham crust (made with regular graham crackers!) and all drizzled in a punchy, caramel-esque cajeta. Mexican cajeta is the sexy, tangy cousin of caramel and dulce de leche, the defining difference being that it's made with goat's milk. The addition of goat's milk gives it an extra, and very welcome, tang. This cheesecake is equally delicious sans cajeta and with either caramel (page 174), dulce de leche (page 179), chocolate ganache (page 84) or simply topped with a scoop of crème fraîche.

MAKES 8 TO 10 SERVINGS

FOR THE CRUST

16 whole graham crackers (9 oz [249 g])

4 tablespoons (55 g) light brown sugar, packed

3 tablespoons (18 g) unsweetened Dutch-process cocoa powder, sifted

½ teaspoon sea salt

8 tablespoons (113 g) unsalted butter, melted

FOR THE CHEESECAKE

1½ cups (255 g) dark chocolate, finely chopped

2 teaspoons (4 g) finely ground espresso

16 ounces (452 g) cream cheese, room temperature

1 cup (220 g) light brown sugar, packed

3 large eggs, room temperature

1 large egg yolk, room temperature

16 ounces (454 g) sour cream, room temperature

1 tablespoon (13 g) vanilla paste or real vanilla extract

½ teaspoon sea salt

For the Crust: Preheat the oven to 350°F (177°C). Grease a 9-inch (23-cm) nonstick springform pan and line with parchment paper.

Put the graham crackers and brown sugar in a food processor or high-speed blender and pulse until the mixture becomes a very fine crumb. Add in the cocoa powder and sea salt and pulse to combine. Drizzle the butter on top and pulse until just mixed and it resembles wet sand. Firmly press the mixture evenly into the bottom of the springform pan. Place the crust in the oven for 10 to 12 minutes or until it starts to turn golden and bronzed around the edges. Set aside to cool completely.

For the Cheesecake: Increase the oven temperature to 400°F (200°C) and place a heat-safe skillet on the lowest rack. Bring 4 cups (1 L) of water to a boil and set aside while you prepare the cheesecake.

In a medium, heat-safe bowl, add the chocolate and ground espresso and set over a medium saucepan of simmering water. Do not let it touch the water or let the water come to a boil. Set a towel on the countertop and once melted, remove from the heat, set on top of the towel and continue stirring until cooled. Set aside.

In the bowl of an electric stand mixer fitted with the paddle attachment, mix the cream cheese and sugar on low for about 2 minutes or until smooth and lump free. Frequently use a spatula to scrape down the sides and bottom of the bowl to make sure everything is incorporated.

In a small bowl, lightly whisk the eggs and egg yolk and then slowly stream them into the bowl with the mixer on low. Continue with the mixer on low for 2 minutes or until combined. Add the sour cream, vanilla and salt and mix on low for another 2 minutes or until well blended. With the mixer still on low, slowly stream in the melted chocolate. Grab a spatula and scrape the sides and bottom of the bowl to make sure it is thoroughly combined. Press through a fine-mesh sieve into the cooled crust, smoothing the top with an offset spatula or the back of a spoon.

(continued)

DARK CHOCOLATE CAJETA CHEESECAKE (CONT.)

FOR THE CAJETA

1¾ cups (420 g) whole goat's milk

⅔ cup (128 g) granulated sugar

½ vanilla bean, split and seeds scraped

½ teaspoon sea salt

¼ teaspoon baking soda

NOTE: Make sure you allow enough time for the cheesecake and cajeta to thoroughly chill and set. This is the perfect make-ahead dessert!

Place the cheesecake in the center of the oven and pour the hot water into the skillet on the bottom rack and quickly shut the oven door. Bake the cheesecake for 15 minutes and then reduce the oven to 250°F (121°C) and bake for an additional 40 to 45 minutes more. When done, the center will jiggle when gently shaken and the edges will be set. Turn off the oven and let the cheesecake sit in the oven for 30 minutes, with the door ajar. After 30 minutes take the cheesecake out of the oven. Let it sit at room temperature for about 1 hour. When cool, wrap tightly (still in the springform pan) and place in the fridge to set overnight.

For the Cajeta: In a large, heavy-bottomed saucepan, whisk together the milk, sugar, vanilla bean seeds and pod and salt and bring to a boil. Reduce to a simmer, whisk in the baking soda and set a timer for 40 minutes. Whenever you walk by the pot, give it a stir and adjust the temperature to keep it from boiling; you just want some bubbles around the edges of the pan. Usually around the 30-minute mark, the color starts to deepen and the mixture begins to thicken a bit. When this happens, it's going to be more prone to a heavy boil (which is bad), so stick near it, adjusting the temperature as necessary and stirring more frequently. You want the cajeta to have a nice thick consistency as well as a bronzed, deep caramel appearance. Strain the cajeta into a lidded, heat-safe container and stash in the fridge until ready to use. It will thicken as it cools.

To Assemble: Remove the cheesecake from the pan and set on a serving plate. Pour the cajeta over the top of the cheesecake and serve.

"Nothing says
'I came here to win'
like jazz hands."

—James Ramsay

MEGA **JAZZ HANDS**
Cakes with Flair

I love a good jazzy cake. I'm thinking layers and swirls, fillings and toppings. Just generally a good case of flair. These are not only beautiful to look at, but beautiful to taste with flavors that range from pineapple curd (page 103) and fresh raspberry ice cream (page 109) to champagne buttercream (page 121) and, my love letter to Argentina, the I Love Argentina Alfajores Cake (page 115) with lots of dulce de leche and chocolate and mega jazz hands. Did I mention there are TWO ice cream cakes in this chapter?

Before we embark on adding some sparkle to our lives, I want to offer some jazz hands tips:

1) Make as much as possible ahead of time so that you're not exhausted or feeling rushed the day of your celebration. Most cake components can be made ahead of time, including cake layers, buttercreams, curds, ice cream, dulce de leche, simple syrups, etc. I like to do the whipped creams and meringues the same day.

2) Read through the recipe completely. Is there any special equipment you need? Borrow it or get it before you get started. Gather all of your ingredients and make sure you have enough of everything.

3) When reading through recipes, make sure you take note of the time involved in making them. Both the ice cream base and the finished ice cream need hours of chill time; curds need time to thoroughly chill in the fridge as well. This will be frustrating if you try to cram it all in on one day and will feel like a breeze if you do the work over several days.

4) Lastly, don't be limited by my designs. I said in the beginning, I go for simple, classic cakes. Any of these cakes could be jazzed up simply with sprinkles and flowers like in the photos or you can go for more flair with edible gold leaf (page 123) and chocolate curls (page 31).

I hope these cakes make your celebrations with friends and family as delicious as ours!

GAVIN'S ICE CREAM CEREAL CAKE

Gavin and I both LOVE cereal, especially Fruity Pebbles™. If you do too, you will love this cake, as it tastes just like a bowl of Fruity Pebbles. The ice cream base will need to chill thoroughly and once assembled, you'll want the cake to chill in the freezer before cutting, so make some room in there and allow for these periods of respite in your ice cream cake planning. I like to make this in a 9-inch (23-cm) round cake pan; if you use a different pan you will need to adjust the bake time accordingly. I think this would be the sweetest birthday cake!

MAKES 10 TO 12 SERVINGS

FRUITY PEBBLES ICE CREAM

1 cup (240 g) whole milk

¾ cup (150 g) granulated sugar

1 cup (240 g) heavy whipping cream

2 large eggs

1 teaspoon (4 g) vanilla paste or real vanilla extract

2 cups (72 g) Fruity Pebbles Cereal

4 to 5 drops Americolor® Gel in Electric Pink (optional)

FOR THE CAKE

2 cups (400 g) granulated sugar

12 tablespoons (170 g) unsalted butter, room temperature, cut into 12 pieces

5 large eggs, room temperature

¾ cup (180 g) sour cream, room temperature

1 tablespoon (15 g) vanilla paste or pure vanilla extract

2 cups plus 3 tablespoons (297 g) all-purpose flour

¾ cup (27 g) Fruity Pebbles Cereal, finely ground

1 teaspoon (5 g) baking powder

1 teaspoon (5 g) baking soda

1 teaspoon (6 g) sea salt

For the Fruity Pebbles Ice Cream: To a medium, heavy-bottomed saucepan, add the milk and granulated sugar and whisk over medium heat until the sugar is dissolved. Take off of the heat and whisk in the cream, eggs and vanilla. Stir in the cereal and pour into a lidded container and stash in the fridge until cool to the touch, for at least several hours or, ideally, overnight.

Strain the ice cream into a clean bowl, pressing as much liquid out of the cereal as possible. Discard the cereal. Add the Americolor® Gel (optional) to brighten up the color; whisk well. Proceed with the instructions for your ice cream maker. Place in a lidded container and freezer to firm up a bit.

For the Cake: Preheat the oven to 350°F (177°C). Grease two 8-inch (20-cm) round cake pans and line with parchment paper. Set aside.

Add the sugar and butter to the bowl of an electric stand mixer fitted with the paddle attachment and mix on medium for 4 to 5 minutes or until light and fluffy. With the mixer on low, add in the eggs, one at a time, making sure each is well blended before adding the next. Add in the sour cream and vanilla and run the mixer for 1 minute more or until fully mixed. In a medium bowl whisk together the flour, finely-ground Fruity Pebbles, baking powder, baking soda and salt and add to the butter mixture in two batches, mixing each until just combined. Divide evenly between the prepared pans and bake in the center of the oven for 35 to 40 minutes. Let sit for 10 minutes before turning out onto a rack to finish cooling.

Line a baking sheet or plate with plastic wrap and make sure that whichever you choose will fit in your freezer. Place one cake layer on top and smear the ice cream evenly over the cake. If the ice cream is too firm, stir to soften it up a bit. Place the second cake layer on top and wrap the cake in the plastic wrap, using more if necessary. Place back in the freezer for several hours (and up to several days) to set.

(continued)

**FOR THE FRUITY PEBBLES
WHIPPED CREAM**

1½ cups (360 g) heavy whipping
cream, cold

4½ tablespoons (32 g) confectioners'
sugar

1 cup (36 g) Fruity Pebbles Cereal

For the Fruity Pebbles Whipped Cream: Place the cold heavy whipping cream in the bowl of an electric stand mixer fitted with the whisk attachment. Whisk on medium until soft peaks form. Sprinkle the confectioners' sugar over the top and whisk until soft peaks return, taking care not to overbeat the cream. Fold the cereal into the whipped cream.

To Assemble: Set the cake on a serving plate and pile high with the whipped cream. Let the cake sit for 5 minutes. Run a sharp knife under warm water, dry it and cut through the cake, repeating between slices.

NOTES: If you don't have an ice cream maker, you can strain the ice cream base into a lidded container, place in the freezer and every 20 minutes vigorously whisk (or use a handheld blender) to break up any ice. Repeat until you've reached the desired consistency. If you use an alternative-sized bake pan, you will need to adjust your bake time. Make the whipped cream just prior to serving.

To grind up the Fruity Pebbles, place them in a food processor fitted with the blade attachment or in a high-speed blender and pulse until reduced to a fine mixture and no large clumps remain.

DAD'S OLIVE OIL-COCONUT LAYERED CAKE
WITH PINEAPPLE CURD

I love a good cake-curd combo, if you haven't caught the gist of this yet. It makes it even better when the cake involved is teeming with olive oil and coconut and is oh-so-flipping-delicious. I first made this cake years ago and posted it on social media, and I think it's my most requested recipe ever. I love the original photo, as the cake looks so incredibly fluffy and Stella is holding a fork and just about to plunge into it. I have been promising to put the recipe on my site for years, but when I started to write this book, I knew this one had to be in here. It's rich, elegant, soft and bright. I'm so happy to be sharing it with you!

MAKES 8 TO 10 SERVINGS

FOR THE PINEAPPLE CURD
⅔ cup (150 g) canned 100% pineapple juice, unsweetened (do not use fresh)

¾ cup (150 g) granulated sugar

¼ cup (30 g) confectioners' sugar

2 large eggs

3 large egg yolks

2 tablespoons (28 g) fresh lemon juice

7 tablespoons (98 g) unsalted butter, room temperature, cut into 7 pieces

FOR THE CAKE
2 cups (400 g) granulated sugar

½ cup (113 g) unsalted butter, room temperature

¼ cup (8 g) lemon zest (3 to 4 lemons)

5 large eggs, room temperature

½ cup (112 g) good-quality extra-virgin olive oil

1½ teaspoons (6 g) vanilla paste or real vanilla extract

1 teaspoon (4 g) coconut extract

3¼ cups plus 2 tablespoons (420 g) cake flour

1 teaspoon (5 g) baking soda

1 teaspoon (6 g) sea salt

1 cup (240 g) buttermilk, shaken and room temperature

1½ cups (75 g) unsweetened coconut, finely shredded

For the Pineapple Curd: Add the pineapple juice to a medium, heavy-bottomed saucepan, bring to a boil and then reduce to a simmer for 5 minutes or until reduced by half (so you'll have ⅓ cup [75 g] of juice remaining). Take off of the heat and whisk in the granulated sugar, confectioners' sugar, eggs, egg yolks and lemon juice. Place back over medium heat and whisk for 5 to 7 minutes or until it starts to thicken, and your whisk feels some resistance. Immediately take off of the heat and slowly whisk in the butter, 1 tablespoon (14 g) at a time, making sure each is completely melted before adding in the next. Press the curd through a fine-mesh sieve and into a heat-safe bowl, cover the surface with plastic wrap and place in the fridge to cool completely.

For the Cake: Preheat your oven to 350°F (177°C). Grease two 8-inch (20-cm) round cake pans and line with parchment paper.

In the bowl of an electric stand mixer fitted with the paddle attachment, add the sugar, butter and lemon zest and mix on medium until light and fluffy, 4 to 5 minutes. With the mixer on low, add the eggs, one at a time, making sure that each is well blended before adding the next. Slowly stream in the oil and mix for 1 minute or until combined. Mix in the vanilla and coconut extract and take the bowl out of the mixer. Set aside.

In a medium bowl, whisk together the cake flour, baking soda and sea salt. Alternate adding the flour and buttermilk to the creamed butter in two batches. Fold in the coconut and evenly divide the batter between the prepared pans. Gently tap the pans on the counter several times to release any trapped air bubbles and smooth the tops. Bake in the center of the oven for 38 to 43 minutes or until the edges are lightly bronzed and the center bounces back when gently pressed. Set the pans on a cooling rack. After 10 minutes, run a knife around the edges and turn the cakes out onto the rack to finish cooling; discard the parchment paper.

(continued)

DAD'S OLIVE OIL-COCONUT LAYERED CAKE
WITH PINEAPPLE CURD (CONT.)

FOR THE CREAM CHEESE COCONUT FROSTING

8 ounces (226 g) cream cheese, room temperature

½ cup (113 g) unsalted butter, room temperature

1 teaspoon (4 g) coconut extract

5½ cups (660 g) confectioners' sugar

1 tablespoon (15 g) whole milk, maybe more to thin

TO GARNISH

1½ cups (75 g) coconut, finely shredded (sweetened or unsweetened)

For the Cream Cheese Coconut Frosting: In the bowl of an electric stand mixer fitted with the paddle attachment, add the cream cheese and butter and beat on medium until they are completely smooth and blended. Add in the coconut extract and confectioners' sugar and mix on low until combined, 1 to 2 minutes. Turn the mixer to medium speed and run for 1 to 2 minutes more, or until the buttercream looks light and whipped. If necessary, add the 1 tablespoon (15 g) of milk to thin.

To Assemble: Set one layer upside down on a cake plate and pipe frosting along the outer edge of the cake as well as some in the center. Fill the remaining space with the pineapple curd (you won't use all of the curd). Add the second layer and cover the tops and sides with the remaining frosting. Grab a handful of coconut and gently press it into the sides and top edge of the cake. Cover the top with more pineapple curd and serve any left over on the side. Add the pineapple curd just prior to serving.

> **NOTE:** This cake is also pretty when garnished with pineapple flowers (page 152).

BUFFALO MILK SWISS ROLL

Buffalo Milk is also known as the official drink of Catalina Island! I grew up in Long Beach, just a short 26 miles across the channel from Catalina. I have so many incredible memories tied to that beautiful place and a lot of them are connected to this gem of a cocktail that is probably more of a liquid dessert than anything else. The original cocktail is a combination of crème de cocoa, crème de banana, Kahlúa®, vodka and half-and-half, and it's topped with whipped cream, nutmeg and a slice of banana—it's heaven. This cake is dedicated to Tina, Wendy, Sally and Keith for showing me the fine art of sailing and cocktailing! Look up the recipe online and enjoy a Buffalo Milk while you make this cake—you'll love it!

MAKES 12 SERVINGS

FOR THE CAKE

5 large eggs, separated

⅔ cup (133 g) granulated sugar, divided

4 tablespoons (57 g) unsalted butter, melted and cooled

1 tablespoon (14 g) vanilla paste or real vanilla extract

1 cup (135 g) all-purpose flour

½ teaspoon baking soda

¾ teaspoon baking powder

½ teaspoon sea salt

FOR THE BUFFALO MILK SOAK

¼ cup (60 g) whole milk

¼ cup (50 g) granulated sugar

1 tablespoon (14 g) crème de cocoa

1 tablespoon (14 g) crème de banana

1 tablespoon (14 g) Kahlúa

1 tablespoon (14 g) vodka

For the Cake: Preheat the oven to 350°F (177°C). Grease a 10 x 15–inch (25 x 38–cm) rimmed baking sheet and cover with a layer of parchment paper. Grease the parchment paper as well. Cut another piece of parchment the size of the pan and set aside.

In the bowl of an electric stand mixer fitted with the whisk attachment, whisk together the egg yolks, ⅓ cup (67 g) of sugar, melted butter and vanilla and beat on medium until light and smooth, about 3 minutes. Transfer to a large bowl and set aside. Clean and dry the whisk attachment and mixing bowl.

In the same bowl of an electric stand mixer fitted with the whisk attachment, add the egg whites and whisk on medium for 1 to 2 minutes or until frothy and opaque. With the mixer on low, slowly stream in the remaining ⅓ cup (67 g) of sugar over the course of 1 minute. Turn the mixture up to high and whisk for about 1 minute more, or until they hold stiff peaks.

In a small bowl, whisk together the flour, baking soda, baking powder and salt. Add to the egg yolk mixture and blend well. Fold in the egg whites in three batches, taking care not to deflate them but also making sure that there are no lumps of meringue. Spread the mixture in an even layer, about ¼ to ½ inch (6 mm to 1.3 cm) thick, into the shape of a rectangle (it doesn't have to be perfect) and onto the prepared baking sheet. Bake in the center of the oven for 12 to 14 minutes.

Dust the extra piece of parchment paper evenly and lightly with flour. As soon as the cake comes out of the oven, flip the cake onto the flour-covered parchment paper. Peel the older layer of parchment off of the backside of the cake. Carefully roll the cake up, jelly roll style and let cool.

For the Buffalo Milk Soak: Combine the milk and sugar in a small saucepan and stir over medium-low heat until the sugar has completely dissolved. Whisk in the crème de cocoa, crème de banana, Kahlúa and vodka and set aside to cool a bit. It's strong, but it'll be fine.

(continued)

BUFFALO MILK SWISS ROLL (CONT.)

FOR THE WHIPPED CREAM

1½ cups (360 g) heavy whipping cream, cold

4½ tablespoons (32 g) confectioners' sugar

1 tablespoon (14 g) crème de cocoa

1 tablespoon (14 g) crème de banana

FOR THE BROWN SUGAR BANANA BUTTERCREAM

5 large egg whites, room temperature

1 cup (220 g) light brown sugar, packed

½ teaspoon cream of tartar

½ teaspoon sea salt

24 tablespoons (339 g) unsalted butter, room temperature, cut into 24 pieces

½ cup (144 g) mashed banana (about 1 medium banana)

1 tablespoon (14 g) crème de cocoa

1 tablespoon (14 g) crème de banana

2 teaspoons (10 g) fresh lemon juice

2 teaspoons (8 g) vanilla paste or real vanilla extract

For the Whipped Cream: Place the cold heavy whipping cream in the bowl of an electric stand mixer fitted with the whisk attachment. Whisk on medium until soft peaks form. Sprinkle the sugar over the top and whisk until soft peaks return, taking care not to overbeat the cream. Take the bowl out of the mixer and fold in the crème de cocoa and crème de banana. Unroll the cake and brush with the cake soak and then cover, in an even layer, with the whipped cream. Carefully roll the cake back up, discarding the parchment paper. Place the cake roll seam side down on a flat serving plate, brush with more cake soak (discard any excess) and set in the fridge to chill while you make the buttercream.

For the Brown Sugar Banana Buttercream: Add the egg whites and sugar to the clean bowl of an electric stand mixer and nestle it in a saucepan of simmering water over medium-high heat. Do not allow the bottom of the bowl to touch the water. Whisk until the mixture is thick and frothy, the sugar is melted (rub some between two fingers; if it feels gritty, keep whisking) and it's hot to the touch. This should take about 5 minutes. Ideally you want it to reach 160°F (71°C). Remove the bowl from the heat and transfer it to a stand mixer fitted with the whisk attachment and add the cream of tartar and the salt. Mix on medium-high speed until stiff and glossy and cool to the touch, about 10 minutes (don't rush it). Make sure the meringue is quite stiff and very cool. Make sure the exterior of the bowl is cool to the touch as well. With the mixer on medium add in the butter one piece at a time, letting each fully blend before adding in the next. Add in the banana, crème de cocoa, crème de banana, lemon juice and vanilla and run the mixer for 1 minute more. Grab a spatula and give it some aggressive stirs to knock out any air bubbles.

To Assemble: Cut the ends off of the cake to reveal a nice, clean swirl of cake and whipped cream. Cover the outside of the cake with the banana buttercream using an offset spatula or, as I did in the photos, using a pastry bag fitted with an Ateco 869 tip. Leave the ends of the cake open so you can see the swirl. Store in the fridge until ready to serve.

FRESH RASPBERRY BROWNIE BAKED ALASKA

Baked Alaskas are so elegant looking and also so flipping easy to make! For this one, I have you make fresh raspberry ice cream and rich, decadent brownies for the base. However, this is so adaptable you could easily use store-bought ice cream if you can't be bothered. And while I love the combination of raspberries and brownies, you could also use the Super-Simple New Year's Day Chocolate Cake (page 31) if you're looking for a more traditional cake base or even caramel in place of the raspberries in the ice cream. The possibilities are endless! I hope this recipe inspires you to get a kitchen torch if you don't already have one!

MAKES 10 TO 12 SERVINGS

FOR THE FRESH RASPBERRY ICE CREAM

12 ounces (340 g) fresh raspberries (about 3¼ cups loosely packed)

3 tablespoons (36 g) granulated sugar

2 tablespoons (28 g) fresh lemon juice

1 cup (240 g) whole milk

¾ cup (150 g) granulated sugar

½ vanilla bean, split and scraped, or 2 teaspoons (8 g) vanilla paste or real vanilla extract

1 cup (240 g) heavy whipping cream

2 large eggs

FOR THE BROWNIES

1¾ cups (350 g) granulated sugar

1½ cups (255 g) dark chocolate, finely chopped

8 tablespoons (113 g) unsalted butter, cut into 8 pieces

⅓ cup (75 g) good-quality extra-virgin olive oil

4 large eggs, room temperature

1 tablespoon (15 g) vanilla paste or real vanilla extract

⅔ cup (50 g) unsweetened Dutch-process cocoa powder, sifted

1 teaspoon (6 g) sea salt

1 cup (135 g) all-purpose flour

For the Fresh Raspberry Ice Cream: In a small bowl, combine the raspberries, sugar and lemon juice and set in the fridge until ready to use.

In a medium, heavy-bottomed saucepan set over medium heat, add the milk, sugar and vanilla (place both the vanilla seeds and the bean in the pan), whisking until the sugar is dissolved, 2 to 3 minutes (dip a finger in the milk; if there is any grit keep whisking). Once dissolved, take off of the heat and whisk in the heavy cream and eggs until smooth. Pour into a lidded container and stash in the fridge for several hours or until cool to the touch. When ready, remove the vanilla bean pod and proceed with your ice cream maker's instructions.

While the ice cream is churning, grab an 8-inch (20-cm) bowl and line with plastic wrap, letting the excess hang over the sides (you'll put your ice cream in here). When the ice cream is just about done, add the raspberries (pressing any excess liquid out of the berries before adding) and let churn for 10 seconds more and then turn off the machine. Scoop into the prepared bowl. Smooth the top of the ice cream, cover with more plastic wrap and place in the freezer to firm up.

For the Brownies: Preheat the oven to 350°F (177°C). Grease an 8-inch round (20-cm) cake pan and line with parchment paper.

In a medium heat-safe bowl, add the granulated sugar, chocolate, butter and oil and set over a medium saucepan of simmering water. Do not let the bowl touch the water or let the water come to a boil. Stir frequently until melted and smooth. Place a towel on the counter and set the bowl on top of it. Whisk in the eggs, one at a time, making sure each is well blended before adding in the next. Add in the vanilla, cocoa powder and salt and whisk to thoroughly mix. Fold in the flour until just combined. Pour the batter into the prepared pan and use the back of your spoon to even the top a bit.

Bake on the middle rack of the oven for 25 minutes. When done, it will have a bit of jiggle in the middle, and if you test with a toothpick, a wee bit of batter will coat it. Let it cool in the pan and leave at room temperature until ready to assemble the cake.

(continued)

FRESH RASPBERRY BROWNIE BAKED ALASKA (CONT.)

FOR THE TOASTED MERINGUE

4 large egg whites, room temperature

½ teaspoon cream of tartar

½ teaspoon sea salt

1 cup (200 g) granulated sugar

½ vanilla bean, split and scraped, or 2 teaspoons (8 g) vanilla paste or real vanilla extract

For the Toasted Meringue: Add the egg whites, cream of tartar and salt to the clean bowl of an electric stand mixer fitted with the whisk attachment and mix on medium until the eggs are frothy, about 2 minutes. With the mixer still on medium speed, very slowly add in the sugar. Turn the mixer to medium-high speed until stiff and glossy, 1 to 2 minutes more. Add in the vanilla and run the machine for 30 seconds more to evenly distribute it throughout the meringue.

To Assemble: Take the ice cream out of the freezer and run some warm water on the outside of the bowl to loosen the ice cream a bit (take care not to get any water in your ice cream). Take the brownies out of the pan and place on a cake plate and invert the ice cream on top. Cover evenly with the meringue, making sure no ice cream is visible and use a kitchen torch to bronze it up. Conversely, you can pop it under the broiler for about 1 minute, keeping an eye on it to make sure it doesn't burn. Serve immediately.

NOTE: You can make the ice cream and brownies ahead of time and assemble just prior to serving as the meringue takes no time to whip up. See Gavin's Ice Cream Cereal Cake (page 102) for tips on making ice cream without an ice cream maker.

NEGRONI QUARANTINI CAKE

During quarantine, thanks to Stanley Tucci, I fell in love with the Negroni (affectionately called: my Quarantini). For all of the challenges 2020 brought, it also ushered in family charcuterie and cocktail hour. We didn't do it every night, but at least once or twice a week until Stella protested: No more prosciutto! If you've never had a Negroni, first make one. Second, the cocktail is a combination of gin, Campari and sweet vermouth with the most predominant flavor being bittersweet orange, which is what I really wanted to highlight in this colorful cake. I highly recommend a Negroni while you bake your cake; my favorite is 2 ounces (57 g) each of Hendrick's®, Campari and Carpano Antica sweet vermouth gently shaken with ice, strained into a chilled glass and topped with a squeeze of an orange—do it!

MAKES 10 TO 12 SERVINGS

FOR THE CAKE

1⅔ cups (208 g) cake flour

1 tablespoon (15 g) baking powder

6 egg whites, room temperature

1 teaspoon (6 g) sea salt

½ teaspoon cream of tartar

1 cup (200 g) granulated sugar, divided

5 large egg yolks

½ cup (112 g) good-quality extra-virgin olive oil

2 teaspoons (8 g) vanilla paste or real vanilla extract

1 teaspoon (4 g) orange blossom water

⅔ cup (160 g) whole milk, room temperature

For the Cake: Preheat the oven to 350°F (177°C). In a small bowl, whisk together your flour and baking powder. Set aside.

In the bowl of an electric stand mixer fitted with the whisk attachment, add the egg whites, salt and cream of tartar. Make sure the bowl and whisk are freshly cleaned and dried. Whisk on medium until the eggs are foamy and frothy, 1 to 2 minutes, and then slowly add in ½ cup (100 g) of sugar, 1 tablespoon (12 g) at a time. You want the sugar to slowly absorb into the egg whites and build structure. Once the sugar is in the mixture, turn the mixer on high until you reach medium peaks; this should take about 1 minute or less. The meringue will look glossy and the tip will slope a bit when you invert the whisk. The meringue should feel smooth when you rub some between your fingers.

In a medium bowl, whisk together the egg yolks, remaining ½ cup (100 g) of sugar, oil, vanilla extract and orange blossom water until the mixture is thick and opaque, 3 to 4 minutes. Alternate adding the flour and the milk to the egg yolk mixture in two batches. Then, fold the egg whites into the mixture in two batches, being careful not to deflate the egg whites but also making sure there aren't any meringue clumps. Scoop the cake batter evenly into a 9-inch (23-cm) ungreased tube pan (ideally with a removable bottom). Run a knife through the cake batter in a zigzag motion to remove any air pockets and smooth the top with an offset spatula or the back of a spoon.

Bake in the center of the oven for 35 to 40 minutes or until puffed up; the top may be cracked, lightly golden and a toothpick or cake tester inserted into the center of the cake comes out clean. Invert the cake onto a wine bottle (upside down) to finish cooling completely, 1 to 2 hours. Once cool, run a knife along the inner and outer edges of the pan and gently coax the cake out of the pan.

(continued)

NEGRONI QUARANTINI CAKE (CONT.)

FOR THE SOAK

¼ cup (50 g) granulated sugar

¼ cup (56 g) water

1 tablespoon (13 g) Campari

1 tablespoon (13 g) sweet vermouth

1 tablespoon (13 g) gin

FOR THE CAMPARI BUTTERCREAM

1 cup (200 g) granulated sugar

⅔ cup (150 g) water, room temperature

8 large egg yolks

24 tablespoons (344 g) unsalted butter, room temperature, cut into 24 chunks

1–2 tablespoons (13–26 g) Campari or to taste

NOTE: For this recipe, you'll need a 9-inch (23-cm) angel food pan, ideally with a removable bottom and definitely not nonstick. If your angel food pan doesn't have a removable bottom, line with parchment paper to make removing the cake from the pan easier.

For the Soak: Combine the sugar and water in a small saucepan and stir over medium-low heat until the sugar has completely dissolved. Take off of the heat and whisk in the Campari, sweet vermouth and gin and set aside to cool. Once the cake and the soak are cool, gently brush the soak over the entire surface of the cake, allowing time to absorb into the cake. Apply one layer of soak and discard any remaining.

For the Campari Buttercream: Add the sugar and water to a medium, heavy-bottomed saucepan over medium-low heat and cook for 20 minutes or until it reaches 240°F (115°C). The sugar will be completely dissolved, but it should not have changed color. Keep an eye on it so that it doesn't start to darken. Don't stir as you don't want to splash the liquid up the sides of the pan.

When the sugar water is almost ready, add the egg yolks to the bowl of an electric stand mixer fitted with the whisk attachment and whisk on high for 4 minutes, or until they have lightened in color. When the sugar is ready, turn the mixer on medium-low and slowly stream the screaming-hot sugar in toward the side of the bowl; be careful not to hit the whisk. Turn the mixer on high and mix until the bottom of the bowl feels cool. Once cool, turn the mixer down to medium and add in the butter, one chunk at a time, making sure each is completely blended before adding in the next chunk. Add in the Campari (depending on how much flavor you want) and run the mixer for 30 seconds more. Add 1 to 2 drops of AmeriColor gel Super Red to give the buttercream a Negroni vibe; this is optional.

To Assemble: Smooth the buttercream over the top of the cooled cake and serve.

I LOVE ARGENTINA ALFAJORES CAKE

I really do love Argentina; this is no exaggeration. If you have the opportunity, go! While in Argentina I fell in love with *alfajores* (who wouldn't?). They are the most delicious vanilla cookies that sandwich dulce de leche and are often dipped in chocolate. After consulting with my friend and Mendoza travel companion, Kevin Masse, I decided to keep this cake as true in flavor to the original as possible: lots of vanilla, creamy caramel-esque dulce and a nice layer of chocolate ganache. At one point during the trip I said to Kevin, "My life is literally peaking right now." I hope you feel this way while eating this cake.

MAKES 10 TO 12 SERVINGS

FOR THE DULCE DE LECHE

1½ cups (360 g) whole milk

1½ cups (360 g) heavy whipping cream

1 cup (200 g) granulated sugar

½ vanilla bean, split and scraped, or 2 teaspoons (8 g) vanilla paste or real vanilla extract

1 teaspoon (6 g) sea salt

1 teaspoon (5 g) baking soda

FOR THE VANILLA BEAN CAKE

2 cups (400 g) granulated sugar

16 tablespoons (226 g) unsalted butter, room temperature, cut into 16 pieces

½ vanilla bean, split and scraped, or 2 teaspoons (8 g) vanilla paste or real vanilla extract

2 large eggs, room temperature

2 large egg yolks, room temperature

⅔ cup (149 g) mayonnaise such as Hellmann's® or Best Foods®, room temperature

3 cups (405 g) all-purpose flour

1 teaspoon (5 g) baking powder

½ teaspoon baking soda

1 teaspoon (6 g) sea salt

1 cup (224 g) water, room temperature

For the Dulce de Leche: In a large, heavy-bottomed saucepan, whisk together the milk, cream, sugar, vanilla bean seeds and pod and salt and bring to a boil. Reduce to a simmer and whisk in the baking soda. Whenever you walk by the pot, give it a stir and adjust the temperature to keep it from boiling; you just want some bubbles around the edges of the pan. Usually between the 30- to 45-minute mark, the color starts to deepen and the mixture begins to thicken a bit. When this happens, it's going to be more prone to a heavy boil (which you don't want), so stick near it, adjusting the temperature as necessary and stirring more frequently. It should be done around 2 hours. You want the dulce to have reduced and thickened as well as become bronzed with a deep caramel color. Use a fine-mesh sieve to strain the dulce into a heat-safe bowl. You should end up with about 2 cups (536 g) of dulce de leche that, once cooled in the fridge, will have the consistency of caramel rather than a super thick, spreadable dulce de leche. Pour into a lidded container and stash in the fridge until ready to use.

For the Vanilla Bean Cake: Preheat the oven to 350°F (177°C). Grease two 8-inch (20-cm) round cake pans and line with parchment paper. In the bowl of an electric stand mixer fitted with the paddle attachment, add the sugar, butter and vanilla seeds (discard the pod), and mix on medium speed until light and fluffy, about 4 to 5 minutes. With the mixer on low add in the eggs and egg yolks, one at a time, making sure each is well blended before adding in the next. Scrape the sides and bottom of the bowl to make sure everything is incorporated. Add in the mayonnaise and mix for 3 minutes more on medium until light, fluffy and fabulous. Take out of the mixer stand and set aside.

In a medium bowl, whisk together the flour, baking powder, baking soda and salt and whisk to blend completely. Alternate adding the flour mixture and water into the butter mixture in three batches, mixing each until just blended. Scrape the sides and bottom of the bowl to make sure everything is well blended. Evenly divide the batter between the two prepared pans, gently tap on the counter several times to release any trapped air bubbles and smooth the tops. Bake in the center of the oven for 35 to 40 minutes. You'll know the cakes are done when they have pulled away from the sides of the pan and the center is slightly puffed. Transfer to a cooling rack and after 20 minutes invert the cakes, remove the parchment paper and allow to cool completely.

(continued)

I LOVE ARGENTINA ALFAJORES CAKE (CONT.)

FOR THE DULCE DE LECHE BUTTERCREAM

5 large egg whites, room temperature

1 cup (200 g) granulated sugar

3 tablespoons (63 g) light corn syrup

½ teaspoon cream of tartar

½ teaspoon sea salt

24 tablespoons (339 g) unsalted butter, room temperature, cut into 24 pieces

⅓ cup (89 g) dulce de leche (recipe above)

FOR THE GANACHE

1 cup (170 g) dark chocolate, finely chopped

½ cup (120 g) heavy whipping cream

½ teaspoon sea salt

2 teaspoons (8 g) vanilla paste or real vanilla extract

For the Dulce de Leche Buttercream: Add the egg whites, sugar and corn syrup to the clean bowl of an electric stand mixer and nestle it in a saucepan of simmering water over medium-high heat. Do not allow the bottom of the bowl to touch the water. Whisk until the mixture is thick and frothy, the sugar is melted (rub some between two fingers; if it feels gritty, keep whisking) and it's hot to the touch. This should take about 5 minutes. Ideally you want it to reach 160°F (71°C). Remove the bowl from the heat and transfer it to the stand mixer fitted with the whisk attachment and add the cream of tartar and salt. Mix on medium-high speed until stiff and glossy and cool to the touch, about 10 minutes (don't rush it). Make sure the meringue is quite stiff and very cool. Also make sure the bowl is cool to the touch before adding the butter (sometimes I set it in the fridge for 5 minutes to expedite).

With the mixer on medium, add in the butter one piece at a time, letting each fully blend before adding in the next. Take the bowl out of the mixer and fold in ⅓ cup (89 g) of dulce de leche (reserve the rest for cake assembly and serving) until you still see streaks of dulce throughout but it's not completely mixed in.

For the Ganache: In a large heat-safe bowl, add the chocolate, cream and sea salt and set over a medium saucepan of simmering water. Do not let the bowl touch the water or let the water boil. Stir frequently until melted and smooth and then stir in the vanilla. Set aside, stirring frequently until cooled but still pourable.

To Assemble: Place one cake layer upside down on a cake plate. Make a thick border of dulce de leche buttercream along the edge of the cake and add a smaller ring in the center of the cake. In between those, fill with a thin layer of dulce de leche (don't overdo it). Place the other cake layer on top and cover the tops and sides with buttercream. Smooth the ganache over the top of the cake, letting some drip down the sides if you'd like. Let the cake sit for an hour or so before serving so that the dulce de leche can set up. Serve with the remaining dulce de leche on the side.

NOTE: Most traditional dulce de leche recipes use milk only. I include the addition of cream because it gives you a thicker dulce in less time. If you only have milk (or don't want to use cream) you will need to reduce the dulce de leche longer to get a nice, thick dulce to add to the buttercream.

CHOCOLATE HORCHATA MERINGUE CAKE

Sweet Jesus this is one delicious cake. This is a moist layer cake topped with airy clouds of chocolate meringue that become perfectly marshmallow-y where the two meet. I wanted this one to be flavored like my favorite *horchata* from Loquita in Santa Barbara, which has heaps of vanilla, cinnamon and orange. This flavor trio in combination with the varying textures makes this cake out-of-this-world delicious! Make sure you have all of the meringue ingredients ready to go before you put the cake in the oven because those 25 minutes go fast.

MAKES 10 TO 12 SERVINGS

FOR THE CAKE

16 tablespoons (226 g) unsalted butter, room temperature, cut into 16 pieces

2 cups (400 g) granulated sugar

3 tablespoons (6 g) fresh orange zest (about 2 oranges)

1 tablespoon (6 g) cinnamon

½ cup (120 g) milk, room temperature

¾ cup (180 g) sour cream, room temperature

3 large eggs, room temperature

1 tablespoon (13 g) real vanilla extract

2 cups (270 g) all-purpose flour

1 cup (85 g) unsweetened Dutch-process cocoa powder, sifted

1 teaspoon (5 g) baking powder

1 teaspoon (5 g) baking soda

1 teaspoon (6 g) sea salt

½ cup (112 g) hot water

For the Cake: Preheat the oven to 350°F (177°C). Grease a 9 x 13–inch (23 x 33–cm) baking pan and line with parchment paper, letting the excess hang over the sides. Set aside.

In the bowl of an electric stand mixer fitted with the paddle attachment, add the butter, sugar, orange zest and cinnamon and mix on medium speed until light and fluffy, 4 to 5 minutes. With the mixer on low, slowly stream in the milk. Scrape the sides and bottom of the bowl to make sure everything is well blended. Add in the sour cream and mix for 1 minute more until light, fluffy and fabulous. With the mixer on low, add in the eggs, one at a time, making sure that each is well blended before adding in the next. Add in the vanilla and run the machine for 30 seconds more. Take the bowl out of the mixer.

In a medium bowl, whisk together the flour, cocoa powder, baking powder, baking soda and salt and whisk to blend completely. Fold the flour mixture into the butter mixture in three batches, mixing each until almost (but not quite) blended. Finally, pour in the hot water and stir to combine. Scrape the sides and bottom of the bowl to make sure everything is well blended. Pour the batter into the prepared baking dish. Tap on the counter several times to settle the cake batter and release any trapped bubbles. Use a spatula to smooth and even out the top of the cake and bake in the center of the oven for 25 minutes.

(continued)

CHOCOLATE HORCHATA MERINGUE CAKE (CONT.)

FOR THE MERINGUE

6 large egg whites, room temperature

¾ teaspoon cream of tartar

¼ teaspoon sea salt

1 cup (200 g) granulated sugar

¼ cup (30 g) confectioners' sugar

⅓ cup (28 g) unsweetened Dutch-process cocoa powder, sifted

⅓ cup (40 g) dark chocolate, finely chopped

1 tablespoon (2 g) fresh orange zest (about 1 orange)

1 teaspoon (2 g) cinnamon

For the Meringue: First, thoroughly wash and dry the electric stand mixer bowl before proceeding. In the bowl of an electric stand mixer fitted with the whisk attachment, add the egg whites, cream of tartar and salt. Whisk on medium until the eggs are foamy and frothy, 1 to 2 minutes, and then slowly add in the sugar a little bit at a time. You want it to slowly absorb into the egg whites and build structure. Once all of the sugar is in the mixture, turn the mixer on high and just before you reach stiff peaks, add the confectioners' sugar. Run the mixer on low to combine and then increase to high until you reach stiff peaks, which should take less than a minute depending on the speed of your mixer. The meringue will look glossy and hold its shape when you invert the whisk. The tip of the inverted meringue will be just shy of 12 o'clock. It should also feel smooth when you rub some between your fingers.

In a small bowl, whisk together the cocoa powder, dark chocolate, orange zest and cinnamon. Take the bowl out of the stand mixer and gently fold in the chocolate-orange mixture—stop mixing when there are still streaks of chocolate and the meringue appears marbled; if you mix the chocolate in completely it will deflate your meringue.

As soon as the cake comes out of the oven, use a cookie or ice cream scoop to drop mounds of meringue over the top of the hot cake and then use an offset spatula or the back of a spoon to gently cover the surface of the cake with the meringue, making sure it's completely covered. Try not to push through the top of the cake. Make some swoops and swirls with the meringue and pop it back into the oven for 25 to 30 minutes or until a toothpick inserted into the center of the cake comes out with some wet crumbs coating it, but not clumps of uncooked cake batter. The surface may appear cracked, which is perfect.

Let cool on a rack for 20 minutes and then use the parchment overhang to lift the cake out of the baking dish and finish cooling completely on a cooling rack. Serve once cool.

NOTE: You'll have quite a few leftover egg yolks, which you should promptly freeze and save for the next time you have dire pudding, custard or pasta cravings!

CHOCOLATE STOUT CAKE
WITH CHAMPAGNE BUTTERCREAM

I love a good stout cake and what can be better than pairing it with champagne buttercream? Often just made around March for St. Patrick's Day, I'm campaigning for them to make a regular appearance in your life. This one is a moist, rich, not-too-sweet chocolate cake. If I used the word more-ish, I would describe it as such here. You won't be able to stop eating it. For the champagne buttercream, we're going to cook down the champagne to concentrate the flavors and it will turn a beautiful light amber. Since you're only using 1 cup (224 g) of champagne, I highly suggest you pour yourself a glass (or two) while you bake!

MAKES 10 TO 12 SERVINGS

FOR THE CAKE

12 tablespoons (170 g) unsalted butter, room temperature

1 cup (220 g) light brown sugar, packed

1 cup (200 g) granulated sugar

2 tablespoons (28 g) good-quality extra-virgin olive oil

3 large eggs, room temperature

1 tablespoon (13 g) vanilla paste or real vanilla extract

2 cups (270 g) all-purpose flour

1 cup (85 g) unsweetened Dutch-process cocoa powder, sifted

1 teaspoon (5 g) baking powder

1 teaspoon (5 g) baking soda

1 teaspoon (6 g) sea salt

1 cup (240 g) buttermilk, shaken and room temperature

1 cup (224 g) stout beer, room temperature

For the Cake: Preheat the oven to 350°F (177°C). Grease two 8-inch (20-cm) round cake pans and line with parchment paper.

In the bowl of an electric stand mixer fitted with the paddle attachment, add the butter and both sugars and mix on medium until light and fluffy, 4 to 5 minutes. With the mixer on low, add the oil. Periodically scrape the sides and bottom of the bowl to make sure everything is combined. With the mixer on low, add in the eggs, one at a time, making sure each is well blended before adding the next. Add in the vanilla and run the machine for 1 minute more. Take the bowl out of the mixer.

In a medium bowl, whisk together the flour, cocoa powder, baking powder, baking soda and salt. In a large liquid measuring cup, whisk together the buttermilk and beer. Alternate adding the flour and buttermilk mixtures to the bowl with the creamed butter in three batches. Divide evenly between the prepared pans, tapping on the counter to release any trapped air bubbles and smoothing the tops with an offset spatula or the back of a spoon. Bake in the center of the oven for 35 to 40 minutes, or until puffed and the center bounces back when gently pressed. Set the pans on a cooling rack. After ten minutes, run a knife around the edges and turn the cakes out onto the rack to cool completely.

(continued)

CHOCOLATE STOUT CAKE
WITH CHAMPAGNE BUTTERCREAM (CONT.)

FOR THE CHAMPAGNE BUTTERCREAM

1 cup (224 g) champagne

8 ounces (226 g) cream cheese, room temperature

8 tablespoons (113 g) unsalted butter, room temperature

5 cups (600 g) confectioners' sugar

For the Champagne Buttercream: In a medium, heavy-bottomed saucepan, add the champagne and bring to a boil. Reduce the heat to medium and simmer the champagne until it has reduced to about ⅓ cup (75 g); this should take about 10 minutes. Transfer to a heat-safe bowl and cool completely before using.

In the bowl of an electric stand mixer fitted with the paddle attachment, add the cream cheese and butter and mix on medium until completely smooth and combined. Add in the reduced and cooled champagne, running the mixer for 1 minute or until combined. Finally add in the confectioners' sugar and beat on medium until smooth, light and fluffy.

To Assemble: Place one cake layer upside down on a cake plate and cover with an ample amount of buttercream. Place the second layer over the top, right side up, and cover with the remaining buttercream. Use an offset spatula or the back of a spoon to make all of the swoops and swirls.

> **NOTE:** To decorate this cake I used edible gold leaf. It can be a bit fussy to use and tends to stick to things like plastic wrap. To apply, I use a clean, unused paint brush to place little bits around the frosted cake. I often use a toothpick to help navigate the gold leaf off of the brush. Don't reach for perfection, just have fun playing with it. I love how it gives the cake some sparkle and jazz hands.

"Cake baking has to be, however innocently,
one of the great culinary scams:
it implies effort, it implies domestic prowess;
but believe me, it's easy."

—Nigella Lawson

BIG BEAUTIFUL
BUNDTS

I like big, beautiful Bundts, what can I say? In my homage to the Bundt, can we all just agree that they're beautiful straight out of the pan without any glosses or glazes? So, with that in mind, I created two pretty basic Bundts that you can riff on: the Mega Vanilla Cream-Filled Market Cake (page 126) and the Triple Chocolate Threat Cake (page 136). These are great with glazes, without glazes, with a dusting of powdered sugar, a pile of berries or anything else, really. Get frisky with 'em!

Bundts are relatively easy cakes to make; the only tricky part is getting them out of the pan with zero sticking. Here's how you do it:

For greasing a Bundt pan, I prefer nonstick cooking sprays. For best results, use a baking spray with flour or "perfect release" on the label (NordicWare makes a fabulous one called Baker's Joy®). When spraying your pan, use light, even strokes and don't let it pool at the base of the pan. If using a cooking spray without flour, then I highly recommend lightly coating the pan with either flour (for vanilla or light-colored cakes) or unsweetened cocoa powder (for chocolate cakes). Put 2 tablespoons (18 g all-purpose flour or 10 g cocoa powder) of either in the pan and tap around to thoroughly coat the interior of the pan. Discard the excess.

Don't prepare your Bundt pan until just prior to using; I have you do it this way in each recipe.

Look for nice, sturdy Bundt pans that are ideally nonstick. All of the Bundts used for these recipes are in the 12- to 15-cup (2.8- to 3.5-L) range. If you use a Bundt pan that's on the smaller side, don't fill it more than three-fourths full and place a baking sheet beneath to catch any overflow.

Once out of the oven, let your Bundt cool for 10 minutes on a rack before using a thin spatula or knife to gently loosen it from the sides and center of the pan. Invert the cake, let sit for 1 minute, remove the pan and then finish cooling. Don't wait longer than 10 minutes, as you run the risk of it sticking to the pan.

Armed with these tips you'll be churning out big, beautiful Bundts consistently! If you're a lover of banana bread, I cannot recommend the Banana Rum Cake (page 129) enough; it's a slice of heaven! If you're looking for a quickie birthday cake, check out the Triple Chocolate Threat Cake (page 136), which is pretty much identical to the birthday cake my mom's been making me my entire life. And if you love s'mores as much as I do, check out Gavin's S'mores Cake (page 141) and live your best life!

There is a lot of ganache drizzle happening in this chapter! Feel free to mix it up and look to the Casual Cakes chapter (page 53) for more drizzle options.

MEGA VANILLA CREAM-FILLED MARKET CAKE

These are reminiscent of the cream-filled treats of our youth . . . you know, the ones that came as spongy logs, wrapped in plastic, from the corner market. This one hints to its past but shines on its own with a dense, moist mega vanilla cake base that's filled with marshmallow cream and dusted in powdered sugar.

MAKES 8 TO 10 SERVINGS

FOR THE CAKE

2 cups (400 g) granulated sugar

1 vanilla bean, split and seeds scraped

16 tablespoons (226 g) unsalted butter, room temperature, cut into 16 pieces

3 large eggs, room temperature

1 cup (224 g) water, room temperature

⅔ cup (160 g) sour cream, room temperature

1 tablespoon (14 g) fresh lemon juice

2 teaspoons (10 g) baking powder

1 teaspoon (5 g) baking soda

1 teaspoon (6 g) sea salt

3 cups (405 g) all-purpose flour, plus more for the pan

FOR THE MARSHMALLOW CREAM

3 large egg whites, room temperature

¾ cup (150 g) granulated sugar

2 tablespoons (42 g) light corn syrup

¼ teaspoon cream of tartar

¼ teaspoon sea salt

1 vanilla bean, split and seeds scraped, or 1 tablespoon (13 g) vanilla paste or real vanilla extract

TO GARNISH

Confectioners' sugar

For the Cake: Preheat oven to 350°F (177°C).

In the bowl of an electric stand mixer fitted with the paddle attachment, add the sugar and vanilla bean seeds and massage the seeds into the sugar. Add the butter and mix on medium until light and fluffy, 4 to 5 minutes. Add in the eggs, one at a time, making sure each is well blended before adding in the next. Scrape the sides and bottom of the bowl to make sure everything is combined.

In a small bowl, whisk together the water, sour cream and lemon juice. Add to the cake batter, along with the baking powder, baking soda and salt and run the machine for 1 minute or until everything is combined. Take the bowl out of the mixer and use a spatula to fold in the flour until just combined, making sure there are no hidden pockets of flour. The cake batter will be thick. Set aside.

For the Marshmallow Cream: Add the egg whites, sugar and corn syrup to the clean bowl of an electric stand mixer and nestle it in a saucepan of simmering water over medium-high heat. Do not allow the bottom of the bowl to touch the water. Whisk until the mixture is thick and frothy, the sugar is melted (rub some between two fingers; if it feels gritty, keep whisking) and it's hot to the touch. This should take about 5 minutes. Ideally, you want it to reach 160°F (71°C). Remove the bowl from the heat, transfer it to the stand mixer fitted with the whisk attachment and add the cream of tartar and salt. Mix on medium-high speed until stiff and glossy and cool to the touch, about 10 minutes (don't rush it). Add in the vanilla and run the machine for 30 seconds more. Set aside.

(continued)

NOTE: You can easily make this a basic vanilla Bundt cake by omitting the marshmallow cream.

Spray a 12- to 15-cup (2.8 to 3.5-L) Bundt pan lightly and evenly to coat it with nonstick cooking or baking spray. Use a fine-mesh sieve to sift 2 tablespoons (18 g) of all-purpose flour evenly over the interior, dumping out the excess. Skip this last step if using a baking spray with flour. Pour half of the batter into the cake pan and then add three-fourths of the marshmallow cream, leaving a gutter along the edges of the Bundt pan. Cover with the remaining cake batter. Tap on the counter several times to release trapped air bubbles. If using the smaller-sized Bundt pan, place a rimmed baking sheet beneath and never fill more than three-fourths full. Bake in the center of the oven for about 50 minutes. Use a toothpick or cake tester to test for doneness. Some moisture and crumbs are fine, but if it's coated in cake batter, bake it for several minutes more. Another way to test for doneness: press the center part of the cake gently, and it should spring back.

Let the cake sit for 10 minutes on a cooling rack. After 10 minutes, gently run a knife or thin spatula along the rim of the pan, as well as the center tube, to release the cake from the pan. Invert a cooling rack over the top of the pan and then flip the whole thing over, so that the cake gently falls onto the cooling rack, right side up. Let sit for 1 minute and then slowly lift the pan off of the cake and let cool on the rack.

To Garnish: Dust with confectioners' sugar and decorate with the remaining marshmallow cream (if you'd like).

BANANA RUM CAKE

This is, quite frankly, banana heaven. Bananas are quickly sauteed in butter, brown sugar and rum and then folded into a moist, banana-rich buttermilk cake batter. The whole lot is then covered in a brown butter rum drizzle. Literally, all of my favorite things. So many good flavors happening here, so many delicious caramel and banana notes, this one is destined to become your new favorite way to use sugar-spotted bananas!

MAKES 8 TO 10 SERVINGS

FOR THE RUM BANANAS

2 tablespoons (28 g) unsalted butter

1½ cups (345 g) ripe bananas peeled and small diced (about 3 small bananas)

¼ cup (55 g) dark brown sugar, packed

2 tablespoons (28 g) dark rum

FOR THE CAKE

1 cup (220 g) dark brown sugar, packed

1 cup (200 g) granulated sugar

8 tablespoons (113 g) unsalted butter, room temperature

1 teaspoon (2 g) nutmeg

3 large eggs, room temperature

½ cup (112 g) good-quality extra-virgin olive oil

¾ cup (171 g) coarsely mashed bananas (about 1½ bananas)

1 tablespoon (13 g) vanilla paste or real vanilla extract

3 cups (405 g) all-purpose flour, plus more for the pan

1½ teaspoons (8 g) baking soda

1 teaspoon (6 g) sea salt

1 cup (240 g) buttermilk, shaken and room temperature

For the Rum Bananas: In a medium skillet set over medium-high heat, melt the butter. Add the bananas and sprinkle with the brown sugar, tossing to coat, but don't over-fuss with them. Let cook for 1 minute. Add the rum and cook for 1 minute more. Pour into a heat-safe bowl to cool. Set aside.

For the Cake: Preheat the oven to 350°F (177°C).

In the bowl of an electric stand mixer fitted with the paddle attachment, add the brown sugar, granulated sugar, butter and nutmeg and mix on medium until light and fluffy, 4 to 5 minutes. With the mixer on low, add in the eggs, one at a time, making sure each is well blended before adding in the next. Scrape the sides and bottom of the bowl to make sure everything is combined. With the mixer on low, slowly stream in the oil until it is completely blended. Add in the mashed bananas and vanilla and run the machine for 30 seconds more. Take the bowl out of the mixer and set aside.

In a medium bowl, whisk together the flour, baking soda and salt. Alternate adding the flour and the buttermilk to the butter mixture in two batches, mixing each addition until just barely combined. Fold in the rum bananas, leaving any excess liquid in the bowl.

Spray a 12- to 15-cup (2.8- to 3.5-L) Bundt pan lightly and evenly with nonstick cooking or baking spray. Use a fine-mesh sieve to sift 2 tablespoons (18 g) of all-purpose flour evenly over the interior, dumping out the excess. Skip this last step if using baking spray with flour. Pour the batter into the cake pan, gently tapping the pan on the counter several times to release trapped air bubbles and smoothing the top with an offset spatula or the back of a spoon. Bake in the center of the oven for 55 to 60 minutes. Use a toothpick or cake tester to test for doneness. Some moisture and crumbs are fine, but if it's coated in cake batter, bake it several minutes more. Another way to test for doneness: press the center of the cake gently and it should spring back when your finger lifts.

(continued)

BANANA RUM CAKE (CONT.)

FOR THE BROWN BUTTER RUM DRIZZLE

4 tablespoons (57 g) unsalted butter

1½ cups (180 g) confectioners' sugar, sifted

3 tablespoons (39 g) dark rum

Let the cake sit for 10 minutes on a cooling rack. After 10 minutes, gently run a knife or thin spatula along the rim of the pan, as well as the center tube, to release the cake from the pan. Invert the cooling rack over the top of the pan and then flip the whole thing over, so that the cake gently falls onto the cooling rack, right side up. Let it sit for 1 minute and then slowly lift the pan off of the cake and let cool on the rack.

For the Brown Butter Rum Drizzle: Place the butter in a small, heavy-bottomed saucepan and melt over medium heat. Once melted, crank up the heat to medium-high. Continue stirring for 2 to 3 minutes and look for small bronze bits settling on the bottom of the pan. Once this happens, take it off the heat and pour it into a medium, heat-safe bowl and let sit for 5 to 10 minutes or until cool to the touch. Whisk in the confectioners' sugar and rum until smooth. Drizzle over the top of the cake and serve.

NOTE: I tested this with bourbon and rum; both are fabulous!

COZY APPLE SOUR CREAM CAKE
WITH APPLE CIDER DRIZZLE

In this recipe, apples get tossed with brown sugar and spices and while you throw the cake together, all of those fabulous flavors mingle together. The cake base is fluffy, moist and spiced with cinnamon and nutmeg. This one is so perfect with the apple cider drizzle and is equally fabulous with just a dusting of confectioners' sugar.

MAKES 8 TO 10 SERVINGS

FOR THE APPLES

2 cups (250 g) apples, unpeeled and small diced

2 tablespoons (28 g) light brown sugar, packed

1 tablespoon (9 g) all-purpose flour

½ tablespoon (7 g) fresh lemon juice

¾ teaspoon cinnamon

¼ teaspoon nutmeg

FOR THE CAKE

1 cup (220 g) light brown sugar, packed

1 cup (200 g) granulated sugar

8 tablespoons (113 g) unsalted butter, room temperature

1 teaspoon (2 g) cinnamon

½ teaspoon nutmeg

3 large eggs, room temperature

½ cup (112 g) sunflower or grapeseed oil

1 cup (240 g) sour cream, room temperature

1 tablespoon (14 g) vanilla paste or real vanilla extract

3 cups (405 g) all-purpose flour, plus more for the pan

2 teaspoons (10 g) baking powder

1 teaspoon (5 g) baking soda

1 teaspoon (6 g) sea salt

¾ cup (168 g) unsweetened apple cider or juice, room temperature

FOR THE APPLE CIDER GLAZE

1½ cups (180 g) confectioners' sugar, sifted

2 tablespoons (30 g) heavy whipping cream

2 tablespoons (26 g) apple cider

For the Apples: In a medium bowl, combine the apples, sugar, flour, juice, cinnamon and nutmeg, tossing to combine. Set aside.

For the Cake: Preheat the oven to 350°F (177°C). In the bowl of an electric stand mixer fitted with the paddle attachment, add the brown sugar, granulated sugar, butter, cinnamon and nutmeg and run the mixer on medium until the mixture has lightened in color and texture, 4 to 5 minutes. With the mixer on low, add in the eggs, one at a time, making sure each is well blended before adding in the next. Scrape the sides and bottom of the bowl to make sure everything is well combined. Slowly stream in the oil and run the mixer for 1 minute more. Add the sour cream and vanilla and mix for 1 minute on medium until light and well combined. Take the bowl out of the mixer and set aside.

In a medium bowl, whisk together the flour, baking powder, baking soda and salt. Alternate adding the flour and the cider to the cake batter in two batches, mixing each addition until barely combined. Fold in the apples until evenly distributed.

Spray a 12- to 15-cup (2.8- to 3.5-L) Bundt pan lightly and evenly with nonstick cooking or baking spray. Use a fine-mesh sieve to sift 2 tablespoons (18 g) of all-purpose flour evenly over the interior, dumping out the excess. Skip this last step if using baking spray with flour. Pour the batter into the cake pan, tapping on the counter several times to release trapped air bubbles and smoothing the top with an offset spatula or the back of a spoon. Bake in the center of the oven for 55 to 60 minutes. Use a toothpick or cake tester to test for doneness. Some moisture and crumbs are fine, but if it's coated in cake batter, bake it for several minutes more. Another way to test for doneness is to press the center part of the cake gently, and if it springs back when your finger lifts, it's ready.

Let the cake sit for 10 minutes on a cooling rack. After 10 minutes, gently run a knife or thin spatula along the rim of the pan, as well as the center tube, to release the cake from the pan. Invert the cooling rack over the top of the pan and then flip the whole thing over, so that the cake gently falls onto the cooling rack, right side up. Let it sit for 1 minute and then slowly lift the pan off of the cake and let cool on the rack.

For the Apple Cider Glaze: Whisk together the confectioners' sugar, cream and the apple cider/juice until smooth and drizzle over the top of the cake.

AUNT KATHY'S CARROT CAKE

I love me some carrot cake. It always reminds me of my Aunt Kathy, so I created this cake in her honor. It's loaded with carrots so, drumroll, it's like a full veggie serving. I'm just kidding, I have no idea. I went for a basic carrot cake, no raisins or walnuts to make this a divisive cake (but feel free to add if you love them!), and topped it with a classic cream cheese frosting because what's life without carrot cake and cream cheese?!

MAKES 8 TO 10 SERVINGS

FOR THE CAKE

1 cup (220 g) light brown sugar, packed

1 cup (200 g) granulated sugar

8 tablespoons (113 g) unsalted butter, room temperature

1 tablespoon (6 g) cinnamon

½ teaspoon nutmeg

3 large eggs, room temperature

¾ cup (168 g) sunflower or grapeseed oil

1 tablespoon (14 g) vanilla paste or real vanilla extract

3½ cups (346 g) carrots, peeled and grated (about 5 medium carrots)

3 cups (405 g) all-purpose flour, plus more for the pan

2 teaspoons (10 g) baking powder

1 teaspoon (5 g) baking soda

1 teaspoon (6 g) sea salt

¾ cup (180 g) whole milk, room temperature

FOR THE CREAM CHEESE FROSTING

4 ounces (113 g) cream cheese, room temperature

3 tablespoons (42 g) unsalted butter, room temperature

6 tablespoons (110 g) heavy whipping cream, room temperature

2 cups (240 g) confectioners' sugar, sifted

½ teaspoon sea salt

For the Cake: Preheat the oven to 350°F (177°C).

In the bowl of an electric stand mixer fitted with the paddle attachment, add the brown sugar, granulated sugar, butter, cinnamon and nutmeg and run the machine on medium until everything is light and fluffy, 4 to 5 minutes. With the mixer on low, add in the eggs, one at a time, making sure each is well blended before adding in the next. Scrape the sides and bottom of the bowl to make sure everything is well blended. Slowly stream in the oil, and then add the vanilla and carrots. Take the bowl out of the mixer and set aside.

In a medium bowl, whisk together the flour, baking powder, baking soda and salt. Alternate adding the flour and milk to the butter mixture in two batches, mixing each one until barely combined.

Spray a 12- to 15-cup (2.8- to 3.5-L) Bundt pan lightly and evenly with nonstick cooking or baking spray. Use a fine-mesh sieve to sift 2 tablespoons (18 g) of all-purpose flour evenly over the interior, dumping out the excess. Skip this last step if using baking spray with flour. Pour the batter into the cake pan, tapping on the counter several times to release trapped air bubbles and smoothing the top with an offset spatula or the back of a spoon. Bake in the center of the oven for 50 to 55 minutes. Use a toothpick or cake tester to test for doneness. Some moisture and crumbs are fine, but if it's coated in cake batter, bake it for several minutes more. Another way to test for doneness is to press the center part of the cake gently, and if it springs back when your finger lifts, it's ready.

Let the cake sit for 10 minutes on a cooling rack. After 10 minutes, gently run a knife or thin spatula along the rim of the pan, as well as the center tube, to release the cake from the pan. Invert the cooling rack over the top of the pan and then flip the whole thing over, so that the cake gently falls onto the cooling rack, right side up. Let it sit for 1 minute and then slowly lift the pan off of the cake and let cool on the rack.

For the Cream Cheese Frosting: In the bowl of an electric stand mixer fitted with the paddle attachment, add the cream cheese and butter and run the mixer on medium until light, smooth and completely combined. Add in the cream, confectioners' sugar and salt and mix on low until combined and then increase the speed to medium for 1 to 2 minutes until smooth and completely blended. Smear over the top of the cooled cake and serve.

TRIPLE CHOCOLATE THREAT CAKE

This cake is strictly for chocolate lovers! It is almost exactly the same in taste, texture and style (hello, Bundt!) to the one my mom made me every year growing up (without the box). All it needs is some vanilla ice cream or a glass of cold milk to go along with it.

MAKES 8 TO 10 SERVINGS

FOR THE CAKE

16 tablespoons (226 g) unsalted butter, room temperature, cut into 16 pieces

2 cups (400 g) granulated sugar

3 large eggs, room temperature

⅔ cup (149 g) good-quality mayonnaise such as Hellmann's® or Best Foods®, room temperature

1 tablespoon (13 g) vanilla paste or real vanilla extract

2 cups (270 g) all-purpose flour

1 cup (85 g) unsweetened Dutch-process cocoa powder, sifted (plus more for the pan)

1 teaspoon (5 g) baking powder

½ teaspoon baking soda

1 teaspoon (6 g) sea salt

1 cup (224 g) hot water

1 cup (170 g) dark chocolate chips

FOR THE GANACHE

1 cup (170 g) dark chocolate, finely chopped

1 cup (240 g) heavy whipping cream

½ teaspoon sea salt

2 teaspoons (8 g) vanilla paste or real vanilla extract

TO GARNISH

Sprinkles (optional)

For the Cake: Preheat your oven to 350°F (177°C). In the bowl of an electric stand mixer fitted with the paddle attachment, add the butter and sugar and mix on medium speed until light and fluffy, 4 to 5 minutes. With the mixer on low, add in the eggs, one at a time, making sure each is well blended before adding in the next. Scrape the sides and bottom of the bowl to make sure everything is incorporated. Add in the mayonnaise and vanilla and mix for 3 minutes more on medium until light, fluffy and fabulous. Take out of the mixer stand and set aside. In a medium bowl, whisk together the flour, cocoa powder, baking powder, baking soda and salt and whisk to blend completely. Fold the flour mixture into the butter mixture in three batches, mixing each until almost (but not quite) blended. Finally, pour in the hot water and whisk until combined. Scrape the sides and bottom of the bowl to make sure everything is well blended.

Spray a 12- to 15-cup (2.8- to 3.5-L) Bundt pan lightly and evenly with nonstick cooking or baking spray. Use a fine-mesh sieve to sift 2 tablespoons (10 g) of unsweetened cocoa powder evenly over the interior, dumping out the excess. Skip this last step if using baking spray with flour. Fold the chocolate chips into the cake batter and pour the batter into the cake pan, tapping on the counter several times to release trapped air bubbles and smoothing the top with an offset spatula or the back of a spoon. Bake in the center of the oven for 45 to 50 minutes. Use a toothpick or cake tester to test for doneness. Some moisture and crumbs are fine, but if it's coated in cake batter, bake it for several minutes more. Another way to test for doneness is to press the center part of the cake gently, and if it springs back when your finger lifts, it's ready.

Let the cake sit for 10 minutes on a cooling rack. After 10 minutes, gently run a knife or thin spatula along the rim of the pan, as well as the center tube, to release the cake from the pan. Invert the cooling rack over the top of the pan and then flip the whole thing over, so that the cake gently falls onto the cooling rack, right side up. Let it sit for 1 minute and then slowly lift the pan off of the cake and let cool on the rack.

For the Ganache: In a large heat-safe bowl, add the chocolate, cream and sea salt and set over a medium saucepan of simmering water. Do not let the bowl touch the water or let the water boil. Stir frequently until melted and smooth. Whisk in the vanilla and set aside, stirring frequently until cooled but still pourable.

To Assemble: Line a baking sheet with parchment paper and set the cooled cake, still on the rack, on top of the parchment paper. Drizzle with the cooled ganache, top with sprinkles (if using) and serve.

CHOCOLATE-COCONUT CANDY BAR CAKE

This one takes inspiration from one of my favorite candy bars. This rich chocolate cake has layers of coconut flavor throughout. Coconut milk is used as a liquid in the cake, and then fresh coconut is folded into the batter. A glossy chocolate-almond glaze covers the cake, and if you're feeling it, cover it with more toasted coconut and almond slices. If you're the type of person that digs out Mounds® and Almond Joy® bars from Halloween candy bags, this one's for you!

MAKES 8 TO 10 SERVINGS

FOR THE CAKE

16 tablespoons (226 g) unsalted butter, room temperature, cut into 16 pieces

2 cups (400 g) granulated sugar

3 large eggs, room temperature

⅔ cup (160 g) sour cream, room temperature

½ cup (120 g) full-fat, unsweetened coconut milk, shaken

2 teaspoons (8 g) vanilla paste or real vanilla extract

1 teaspoon (4 g) almond extract

2 cups (270 g) all-purpose flour

1 cup (85 g) unsweetened Dutch-process cocoa powder, sifted (plus more for the pan)

1 teaspoon (5 g) baking powder

1 teaspoon (5 g) baking soda

1 teaspoon (6 g) sea salt

1½ cups (127 g) sweetened shredded coconut (break up any large clumps)

½ cup (112 g) hot, fresh-brewed espresso or strong coffee

For the Cake: Preheat oven to 350°F (177°C).

In the bowl of an electric stand mixer fitted with the paddle attachment, add the butter and sugar and mix on medium until light and fluffy, 4 to 5 minutes. With the mixer on low, add in the eggs, one at a time, making sure that each is well blended before adding in the next. Add in the sour cream and run the mixer for 1 minute. Slowly stream in the coconut milk. Scrape the sides and bottom of the bowl to make sure everything is well blended. Add in the vanilla and almond extract and run the machine for 30 seconds more. Take the bowl out of the mixer.

In a medium bowl, whisk together the flour, cocoa powder, baking powder, baking soda and salt. Add in the shredded coconut and whisk to blend completely. Fold the flour mixture into the butter mixture in three batches, mixing each until almost (but not quite) blended. Finally, pour in the hot espresso and stir. Scrape the sides and bottom of the bowl to make sure everything is combined. Stir the batter enough that everything is combined but be cautious not to mix too much, as we don't want a tough cake. Set aside.

To prep your 12- to 15-cup (2.8- to 3.5-L) Bundt pan, spray evenly and lightly with cooking or baking spray. Sift 2 tablespoons (10 g) of unsweetened cocoa powder over the top and then rotate the pan to coat it evenly. Discard any excess powder. If using baking spray with flour you don't need to add the cocoa powder to the pan. Pour the batter into the Bundt pan. Tap the pan on the counter several times to settle the cake batter and release any trapped bubbles. Use a spatula to smooth and even out the top of the cake batter. Bake in the center of the oven for about 45 minutes. Use a toothpick or cake tester to test for doneness. Some moisture and crumbs are fine, but if it's coated in cake batter, bake it for several minutes more. Another way to test for doneness is to press the center part of the cake gently, and if it springs back when your finger lifts, it's ready.

(continued)

FOR THE CHOCOLATE-ALMOND GANACHE

1 cup (240 g) heavy whipping cream

1 cup (170 g) dark chocolate, finely chopped

½ teaspoon almond extract

TO GARNISH

More sweetened or unsweetened coconut flakes and/or toasted almond slices

Let the cake sit for 10 minutes on a cooling rack. After 10 minutes, gently run a knife or thin spatula along the rim of the pan, as well as the center tube, to release the cake from the pan. Invert the cooling rack over the top of the pan and then flip the whole thing over, so that the cake gently falls onto the cooling rack, right side up. Let it sit for 1 minute and then slowly lift the pan off of the cake. Let the cake cool completely before coating in ganache. Line a baking sheet with parchment paper and set the cooled cake, still on the rack, on top of the parchment paper.

For the Chocolate-Almond Ganache: Add the cream, chocolate and almond extract to a medium, heat-safe bowl set over a medium saucepan of simmering water. Do not let the water boil or touch the bowl. Stir frequently until almost smooth. Take off of the heat and continue stirring for about 30 seconds or until completely smooth. Pour the ganache evenly over the top of the cake—it will be thick. Pick up the baking sheet and tap it several times on the counter to smooth out the chocolate and encourage it to drip down the sides. Sprinkle with coconut and/or almond slices and serve.

> **NOTE:** If your coconut milk is separated (and it usually is), it's okay. Place in a small saucepan over low heat and stir until it melts. Measure out ½ cup (120 g) and set aside, whisking periodically, to cool before using.

GAVIN'S S'MORES CAKE

Gavin and I share an unrelenting sweet tooth and a love for everything s'mores. This cake was created solely with him in mind (but I know you'll love it too!). It's a rich chocolate cake stuffed with marshmallow fluff and crumbles of graham crackers. It's then layered with more chocolate, more marshmallow fluff and more crumbles of grahams. I resisted the urge to make this more complicated than it needed to be, which is all to say that this comes together in a flash. And why aren't we stuffing all of our cakes with marshmallow fluff?

MAKES 8 TO 10 SERVINGS

FOR THE MARSHMALLOW FLUFF

3 large egg whites, room temperature

¾ cup (150 g) granulated sugar

2 tablespoons (42 g) light corn syrup

½ teaspoon cream of tartar

½ teaspoon sea salt

2 teaspoons (8 g) vanilla paste or real vanilla extract

4 whole graham crackers, finely crushed (2 oz [59 g])

FOR THE CAKE

2 cups (400 g) granulated sugar

8 tablespoons (113 g) unsalted butter, room temperature, cut into 8 pieces

3 large eggs, room temperature

½ cup (112 g) good-quality extra-virgin olive oil

⅔ cup (149 g) sour cream, room temperature

1 tablespoon (13 g) vanilla paste or real vanilla extract

1 cup (85 g) unsweetened Dutch-process cocoa powder, sifted (plus more for the pan)

1½ teaspoons (8 g) baking powder

1 teaspoon (5 g) baking soda

1 teaspoon (6 g) sea salt

2 cups (270 g) all-purpose flour

1 cup (224 g) hot water

For the Marshmallow Fluff: Add the egg whites, sugar and corn syrup to the clean bowl of an electric stand mixer and nestle it in a saucepan of simmering water over medium-high heat. Do not allow the bottom of the bowl to touch the water. Whisk until the mixture is thick and frothy, the sugar is melted (rub some between two fingers; if it feels gritty, keep whisking) and it's hot to the touch. This should take about 5 minutes. Ideally, you want it to reach 160°F (71°C). Remove the bowl from the heat, transfer it to the stand mixer fitted with the whisk attachment and add the cream of tartar and salt. Mix on medium-high speed until stiff and glossy and cool to the touch, about 10 minutes (don't rush it). Add in the vanilla and run the machine for 30 seconds more. Remove one-fourth of the marshmallow and set aside to use for piping over the top of the cake; keep covered. Fold the graham crackers into the remaining three-fourths of the marshmallow until just combined. Set aside.

For the Cake: Preheat the oven to 350°F (177°C).

In the bowl of an electric stand mixer fitted with the paddle attachment, add the sugar and butter and mix for 4 to 5 minutes; it will resemble wet sand. Add in the eggs, one at a time, making sure each is well blended before adding the next. Scrape the sides and the bottom of the bowl periodically to make sure everything is well combined. With the mixer on low, stream in the oil. Add in the sour cream and vanilla and run the machine for 1 minute or until well combined. Add in the cocoa powder, baking powder, baking soda and salt and mix for 1 to 2 minutes. Take the bowl out of the mixer and fold in the flour until barely combined. Pour in the hot water and whisk until just combined. Set aside.

(continued)

GAVIN'S S'MORES CAKE (CONT.)

FOR THE CHOCOLATE GANACHE
1 cup (240 g) heavy whipping cream
1 cup (170 g) dark chocolate, finely chopped

TO GARNISH
Graham crackers, crushed

To prep your 12- to 15-cup (2.8- to 3.5-L) Bundt pan, spray it evenly and lightly with cooking or baking spray. Sift 2 tablespoons (10 g) of unsweetened cocoa powder over the top and then rotate the pan to coat it evenly. Discard any excess powder. If using baking spray with flour, there's no need to add the cocoa powder to the pan. Pour half of the batter into the Bundt pan. Add the batch of marshmallow cream with the graham crackers to the center of the cake, leaving a border around the inner and outer edges of the cake (if the marshmallow is near the edges it will make it harder to get the Bundt out of the pan). Cover the filling with the remaining cake batter. Tap the pan on the counter several times to settle the cake batter and release any trapped bubbles. Use a spatula to smooth and even out the top of the cake batter. Bake in the center of the oven for 45 to 50 minutes. Use a toothpick or cake tester to test for doneness. Some moisture and crumbs are fine, but if it's coated in cake batter, bake it for several minutes more. Another way to test for doneness is to press the center part of the cake gently, and if it springs back when your finger lifts, it's ready.

Let the cake sit for 10 minutes on a cooling rack. After 10 minutes, gently run a knife or thin spatula along the rim of the pan, as well as the center tube, to release the cake from the pan. Invert the cooling rack over the top of the pan and then flip the whole thing over, so that the cake gently falls onto the cooling rack, right side up. Let it sit for 1 minute and then slowly lift the pan off of the cake. Let the cake cool completely before coating in ganache. Line a baking sheet with parchment paper and set the cooled cake, still on the rack, on top of the parchment paper.

For the Chocolate Ganache: Add the cream and chocolate to a medium, heat-safe bowl set over a medium saucepan of simmering water. Do not let the water boil or touch the bowl. Stir frequently until almost smooth. Take off of the heat and continue stirring for about 30 seconds or until completely smooth. Set aside, stirring periodically.

To Assemble: Pour the ganache evenly over the top of the cake—it will be thick. Pick up the baking sheet and tap it several times on the counter to smooth out the chocolate and encourage it to drip down the sides. Sprinkle with more graham crackers. Pipe the remaining marshmallow over the top of the cake. I used an Ateco 807 for large dollops, but lots of marshmallow dots with a French tip would be pretty too. If the marshmallow cream has deflated a bit, re-whip before using. Use a kitchen torch to bronze up the meringue and serve.

"I have a friend whose mantra is 'You must choose.' And I believe the exact opposite: I think you should always have at least four desserts that are kind of fighting with each other."

—Nora Ephron

BABY **CAKES**
Mini Treats for Good Times

I am a sucker for anything mini. Seriously, everything is cuter when petite. These are the types of desserts that are perfect for small dinners with friends, to celebrate special occasions (although the argument could be made that all cakes serve this function) or to take to school events. Baby cakes are fabulous for getting desserts out without having to fuss with slices (such a chore!).

Baby cakes come in several shapes and different sizes:

FREE-FORM CAKES

Petite Caramelized Banana Split Pavlovas (page 146) corner the market on free-form cakes in this book. These are dolloped onto a parchment-lined baking sheet and are in need of zero tools or equipment (no ramekins, no muffin tins) to get them in shape. You can use a large ice cream scoop to portion them out or eyeball the meringue using two spoons.

RAMEKIN CAKES

Several baby cakes, such as the Tropical Pineapple Cakes (page 152), Sanyuanli Passion Fruit–Lime Pudding Cakes (page 155) and the Chocolate Hazelnut Pudding Cakes with Crème Anglaise (page 159), use 8-ounce (226-g) ramekins (I love the Le Creuset® mini cocottes). All of these cakes can be served in the cute ramekins or turned out and served on a plate. I recommend the latter (for all but the passion fruit cakes as they're cuter in the ramekins), as we'll spruce them up even more once out of their baking vessels.

LAYERED CAKES

These cakes take a little more work than the others. But trust me, both the Confetti Party Cakes (page 156) and Chocolate-Espresso Cakes with Burnt Caramel (page 149) are worth it! You can bake these in a 9 x 13–inch (23 x 33–cm) rectangle cake and then cut the smaller cakes out of that using round cookie cutters (or a drinking glass!).

CUPCAKES

Lastly, we have the OG baby cake—the cupcake. The Spiced Brown Sugar Cakes (page 162) and KT's Chocolate Cakes with Raspberry Cream Filling and Chocolate Ganache (page 165) are made with a classic, regular-sized muffin tin.

One last note on baby cakes: Many of the cakes in this book can be made into baby cakes using one of the methods outlined above. When downsizing a recipe, make sure to adjust the bake time accordingly.

Go forth and make some baby cakes!

PETITE CARAMELIZED BANANA SPLIT PAVLOVAS

When I was little, I thought ordering a banana split was the height of sophistication. The whipped cream! The chocolate drizzle! The bananas! The cherry on top! What's not to make you completely happy when eating one? The banana-split-meets-pavlova mash-up was destined to happen. When you add the crispy pavlova with the marshmallow center to all of the flavors and textures that are the banana split, well, it just may be the ultimate dessert. Get frisky and play around with adding boozy berries (page 54) in place of the caramelized bananas or dulce de leche (page 179) in place of the chocolate sauce or in addition to it. The possibilities are endless!

Pavlovas are a great make-ahead dessert. I often keep them in the turned-off oven overnight if using the next day (this only works if you don't live in a humid environment, otherwise make the pavlovas within hours of serving). The chocolate sauce, bananas and whipped cream come together quickly and should be done just prior to serving.

MAKES 6 PAVLOVAS

FOR THE PAVLOVA
5 large egg whites
1 cup (200 g) granulated sugar
1 teaspoon (3 g) cream of tartar
½ teaspoon sea salt
¼ cup (30 g) confectioners' sugar
1 teaspoon (4 g) vanilla paste or real vanilla extract

For the Pavlovas: Preheat the oven to 350°F (177°C). Line a large baking sheet with parchment paper.

Add the egg whites and sugar to the clean bowl of an electric stand mixer and nestle it in a saucepan of simmering water over medium-high heat. Do not allow the bottom of the bowl to touch the water. Whisk until the mixture is thick and frothy, the sugar is melted (rub some between two fingers; if it feels gritty, keep whisking) and it's hot to the touch. This should take about 5 minutes. Ideally, you want it to reach 160°F (71°C). Remove the bowl from the heat, transfer it to the stand mixer fitted with the whisk attachment and add the cream of tartar and salt. Mix on medium-high speed until stiff and glossy and cool to the touch, about 10 minutes (don't rush it). Add the confectioners' sugar and vanilla and run the machine for 1 minute more. Divide into six similar-sized mounds, 4 to 5 inches (10 to 13 cm) wide on the prepared baking sheet. Use the back of a spoon to smooth the sides and create shallow valleys in the middle to hold all of the toppings post-bake.

Place in the center of the oven, immediately reduce the temperature to 200°F (93°C) and bake for 90 minutes. Check midway through the bake time to make sure they aren't browning and are still white. If they're taking on any color, turn the oven down to 180°F (82°C). Once done, let the pavlovas cool completely inside the turned-off oven. When done they should be crispy on the exterior and marshmallow-y in the interior. It should take 2 hours or more for them to cool down completely. Leave in the turned-off oven until ready to serve.

(continued)

FOR THE CHOCOLATE SAUCE

½ cup (85 g) dark chocolate, finely chopped

3 tablespoons (45 g) heavy whipping cream

1 tablespoon (21 g) honey

1 tablespoon (14 g) hazelnut liqueur such as Frangelico®

FOR THE CARAMELIZED BANANAS

2 tablespoons (28 g) unsalted butter

1 cup (230 g) ripe bananas peeled and sliced thick (about 2 small bananas)

2 tablespoons (28 g) light brown sugar, packed

2 tablespoons (28 g) hazelnut liqueur such as Frangelico®

FOR THE WHIPPED CREAM

2 cups (480 g) heavy whipping cream, cold

4½ tablespoons (32 g) confectioners' sugar

TO GARNISH

Maraschino cherries

Chopped hazelnuts (optional)

For the Chocolate Sauce: To a medium, heat-safe bowl add the chocolate, cream and honey and set over a saucepan of simmering water. Don't let the water touch the bottom of the bowl or come to a boil. Stir until the chocolate is almost melted and then take off of the heat and continue to stir until smooth. Add in the Frangelico and periodically stir as the sauce cools.

For the Caramelized Bananas: In a medium skillet set over medium-high heat, melt the butter. Add the bananas and sprinkle with the brown sugar, tossing to coat, but don't over-fuss with them. Let cook for 1 minute. Add the Frangelico and cook for 1 minute more. Pour into a heat-safe bowl to cool. Set aside.

For the Whipped Cream: Place the cold heavy whipping cream in the bowl of an electric stand mixer fitted with the whisk attachment. Whisk on medium until soft peaks form. Sprinkle the confectioners' sugar over the top and whisk until soft peaks return, taking care not to overbeat the cream.

To Assemble: Evenly distribute half the whipped cream among the six pavlovas. Then, add the bananas and the remaining whipped cream. Drizzle with chocolate sauce and top each with a cherry and nuts, if using. Serve immediately.

CHOCOLATE-ESPRESSO CAKES
WITH BURNT CARAMEL

These are petite little cakes made of a coffee-rich, chocolate cake base with layers of burnt caramel French mocha buttercream. YUM. The cakes come together in a pinch; you'll make them in a large baking dish and cut out little rounds. For the buttercream, we'll start by making a traditional French buttercream using half of the melted sugar for the frosting and the remaining to make the burnt caramel. We won't be burning it exactly, but we'll be infusing it with heaps of flavor. I first tasted burnt caramel from Recchiuti and immediately fell in love. You will too . . . it just might become your new favorite way to make caramel!

MAKES 20 PETITE LAYERED CAKES

FOR THE CAKE

2 cups (400 g) granulated sugar

16 tablespoons (226 g) unsalted butter, room temperature, cut into 16 pieces

1 tablespoon (13 g) vanilla paste or real vanilla extract

2 teaspoons (4 g) finely ground espresso

3 large eggs, room temperature

2/3 cup (149 g) sour cream, room temperature

2 cups (270 g) all-purpose flour

1 cup (85 g) unsweetened Dutch-process cocoa powder, sifted

1 teaspoon (5 g) baking soda

½ teaspoon baking powder

1 teaspoon (6 g) sea salt

1 cup (225 g) hot, fresh-brewed espresso or strong coffee

For the Cake: Preheat the oven to 350°F (177°C). Grease a 9 x 13–inch (23 x 33–cm) baking pan and line with parchment paper, letting the excess hang over the sides of the pan. Set aside.

In the bowl of an electric stand mixer fitted with the paddle attachment, add the sugar, butter, vanilla and espresso and mix on medium speed until light and fluffy, 4 to 5 minutes. Add in the eggs, one at a time, making sure each is well blended before adding in the next. Scrape the sides and bottom of the bowl to make sure everything is incorporated. Add in the sour cream and mix for 1 minute more on medium until light, fluffy and fabulous. Take the bowl out of the mixer stand and set aside.

In a medium bowl, whisk together the flour, cocoa powder, baking soda, baking powder and salt and whisk to blend completely. Fold the flour mixture into the butter mixture in two batches, mixing until almost (but not quite) blended. Finally, pour in the hot espresso or coffee and stir until completely combined. Scrape the sides and bottom of the bowl to make sure everything is well blended. Stir the batter enough that everything is combined but be cautious not to mix too much as we don't want a tough cake. Pour the batter into the prepared cake pan, gently tapping the pan on the counter to release any trapped air bubbles and smoothing the top with an offset spatula or the back of a spoon. Bake in the center of the oven for 45 to 50 minutes. Cool for 20 minutes in the pan before transferring to the rack to cool completely. Once cool, invert the cake onto a cutting board and use a 2½-inch (6-cm) cookie cutter and cut out 10 cake rounds. Cut each cake round horizontally, through the middle, using a very sharp knife so you end up with two equal-sized cake layers. Sometimes it helps to put them in the freezer for 10 minutes prior to cutting to help get a really clean cut.

(continued)

CHOCOLATE-ESPRESSO CAKES
WITH BURNT CARAMEL (CONT.)

FOR THE FRENCH MOCHA BUTTERCREAM

1½ cups (300 g) granulated sugar

½ cup (113 g) water, room temperature

6 large egg yolks

⅓ cup (25 g) unsweetened Dutch-process cocoa powder

2 teaspoons (4 g) finely ground espresso

½ teaspoon sea salt

32 tablespoons (452 g) unsalted butter, cut into 32 pieces, room temperature

2 teaspoons (8 g) vanilla paste or real vanilla extract

FOR THE BURNT CARAMEL

½ cup (120 g) heavy whipping cream, room temperature

2 tablespoons (28 g) unsalted butter, room temperature

1 teaspoon (4 g) vanilla paste or real vanilla extract

½ teaspoon sea salt

For the French Mocha Buttercream: To make the filling, add the sugar and water to a medium, heavy-bottomed saucepan over medium-low heat and cook for 20 minutes or until it reaches 240°F (116°C). You don't want it to take on any color during this time, so keep an eye on it and adjust the heat accordingly.

Add the egg yolks to an electric stand mixer fitted with the whisk attachment and whisk on high for 4 minutes, or until they have lightened in color. Turn the mixer on medium-low and slowly stream half of the screaming-hot sugar, keeping it toward the side of the bowl and being careful not to hit the whisk. Set aside the remaining hot sugar still in the saucepan (you'll use it for the caramel). Turn the mixer on high until the bottom of the bowl feels cool. Once cool, turn the mixer down to medium and add in the cocoa powder, espresso and salt and then the butter, one chunk at a time, making sure each chunk is completely blended before adding in the next chunk. Add in the vanilla and mix for 1 minute more. Grab a spatula and give it some good aggressive stirs to knock out any air bubbles. Put the buttercream in a pastry bag fitted with a medium-sized French tip (I used Ateco 865). Set aside.

For the Burnt Caramel: Place the saucepan with the remaining melted sugar over medium heat and wait for the sugar to turn a deep bronze and just start to smoke. Immediately take off of the heat and whisk in the cream (careful, it will hiss and steam when you do this). Whisk in the butter, vanilla and salt until smooth and set aside to cool completely (you can place in the fridge to expedite this, but serve at room temperature).

To Assemble: Place a cake round on a plate and pipe some buttercream over the top. Top with a second cake round, pipe with more buttercream and then drizzle with burnt caramel over the top and serve.

TROPICAL PINEAPPLE CAKES

File this one away for the next time you want to do something super cute but with minimal effort! The topping for these comes together in seconds and is a heavenly combo of brown sugar, butter and pineapple—that's it! If you want to make these really wow your dessert-loving companions, then go the extra mile and make the super easy dried pineapple flowers.

MAKES 6 SERVINGS

FOR THE DRIED PINEAPPLE FLOWERS

6 (⅛- to ¼-inch [3- to 6-mm]) thick fresh pineapple rings

FOR THE TOPPING

3 tablespoons (42 g) unsalted butter, melted

6 tablespoons (84 g) light brown sugar, packed

6 (¼-inch [6-mm]) thick fresh pineapple rings, cored and patted dry

FOR THE CAKE

1 cup (200 g) granulated sugar

2 large eggs, room temperature

¾ cup (168 g) sunflower or grapeseed oil

¾ cup (180 g) full-fat unsweetened coconut milk, shaken

¼ cup (50 g) fresh pineapple, finely minced and patted dry

1½ teaspoons (8 g) baking powder

½ teaspoon baking soda

1 teaspoon (6 g) sea salt

1⅔ cups (225 g) all-purpose flour

For the Dried Pineapple Flowers: Preheat the oven to 200°F (93°C) and place a rack in the lower third of the oven. Pat the pineapple slices dry. Put a cooling rack on top of a rimmed baking sheet and place the pineapple slices on the rack. Bake in the lower third of the oven for about 3 hours or until dried and darkened in color. As soon as you take them out of the oven, place them on the bottom of a drinking glass or an inverted mini muffin tin to help them keep their flower-like shape. They are pliable when warm, so sculpt the pineapple flowers how you want them to look. Once cool, set on top of the finished cakes.

Increase the oven temperature to 350°F (177°C). Grease six 8-ounce (226-g) ramekins.

For the Topping: Put ½ tablespoon (7 g) of melted butter in the bottom of each ramekin, swirling to evenly coat. Sprinkle 1 tablespoon (14 g) of brown sugar evenly over the top of the butter. Nestle a pineapple ring on top and set the ramekins in the fridge.

For the Cake: In a large bowl, whisk together the sugar and eggs until frothy and thick, about 2 minutes. Stream in the oil and whisk until completely blended. Whisk in the coconut milk, pineapple, baking powder, baking soda and salt. Scrape the sides and bottom of the bowl to make sure everything is well combined. Fold in the flour until just combined. Evenly divide the batter among the ramekins until three-fourths full, tapping on the counter to release any trapped air bubbles and smoothing the tops with the back of a spoon, if necessary.

Place the ramekins on a baking sheet and bake in the center of the oven for 30 to 35 minutes or until puffed and lightly bronzed. Set on a cooling rack for 5 minutes and then run a knife around the edge of the cakes and invert onto the cooling rack to cool completely. Garnish with the pineapple flowers and serve.

NOTES: You may need to trim your pineapple rings so that they fit perfectly into your ramekins. Reserve any trimmed pineapple to add to the cake batter. If your coconut milk is separated (it usually is), it's okay. Place in a small saucepan over low heat and stir until melted. Measure and set aside, whisking periodically, to cool before using.

SANYUANLI PASSION FRUIT-LIME
PUDDING CAKES

When we were living in Beijing, we fell in love with passion fruit. We would buy passion fruit by the bagful, noshing on them for breakfast, snacks, anytime. This dessert is a celebration of those memories. I love the bright combination of passion fruit and lime together. Served with barely-sweetened whipped cream and fresh juicy passion fruit pulp, these are perfect any time you can get your hands on some passion fruit!

MAKES 6 SERVINGS

FOR THE CAKES

16 tablespoons (226 g) unsalted butter, melted (plus more for the ramekins)

¾ cup (102 g) all-purpose flour, plus more for the ramekins

6 large eggs, room temperature and separated

1 cup (200 g) granulated sugar, divided

1 tablespoon (2 g) lime zest (1 to 2 limes)

½ cup (112 g) strained fresh passion fruit juice (10 to 15 passion fruits; reserve the seeds and pulp for garnish)

½ teaspoon sea salt

FOR THE WHIPPED CREAM

1½ cups (360 g) heavy whipping cream, cold

4½ tablespoons (32 g) confectioners' sugar

TO GARNISH

Reserved passion fruit seeds and pulp

NOTE: If you can't find fresh passion fruit, use barely sweetened passion fruit juice or puree in place of the fresh passion fruit juice.

For the Cakes: Preheat the oven to 350°F (177°C). Lightly butter six 8-ounce (226-g) ramekins and add 1 tablespoon (9 g) of all-purpose flour to each, tapping and rotating to coat the interior completely with a thin layer of flour. Discard the remaining flour and place the ramekins in a large roasting pan. Boil some water and set aside.

In the bowl of an electric stand mixer fitted with the whisk attachment, add the egg whites (reserve egg yolks for the next step). Make sure the bowl and whisk are freshly cleaned and dried. Whisk on medium for several minutes until the eggs are frothy, and then slowly add ½ cup (100 g) of granulated sugar, 1 tablespoon (13 g) at a time, letting each addition slowly dissolve before adding the next one. This should take 3 to 5 minutes. Turn the mixer on high and whisk for about 1 minute more or until the meringue is shiny, the whisk is leaving track marks in the meringue and the tip of the meringue is sloped (medium peaks) when the whisk is inverted. Take care not to overwhisk the meringue.

In another large bowl, whisk together the egg yolks, remaining ½ cup (100 g) of granulated sugar and lime zest and whisk until thick and pale, about 2 minutes. Whisk in the melted butter, passion fruit juice/puree and salt until thoroughly combined. Mix in the flour until barely combined and then fold in the meringue in three batches. You want to make sure you don't have any clumps of meringue left in the batter while also taking care not to deflate the meringue too much. It's a dance. Evenly distribute the batter among the 6 prepared ramekins, filling each about three-fourths full and gently smoothing the tops. Pour the hot water in the roasting pan, taking care not to get any in the ramekins and filling the water no more than halfway up the sides of the ramekins. Bake in the center of the oven for 20 to 25 minutes; they will be puffed up and may have some cracks, which is fine. Remove from the water bath and set on a wire rack while you prepare the whipped cream.

For the Whipped Cream: Place the cold heavy whipping cream in the bowl of an electric stand mixer fitted with the whisk attachment. Whisk on medium until soft peaks form, 2 to 3 minutes. Sprinkle the confectioners' sugar over the top and whisk until soft peaks return, about 1 minute more.

To Assemble: Top with a dollop of whipped cream and some fresh passion fruit pulp. These are best served slightly warm the day they were made.

CONFETTI PARTY CAKES

What's a party without some confetti cakes? I love how these petite little cakes are baked in a large rectangular baking dish and all you need is a 2½-inch (6-cm) cookie cutter to stamp out the cake rounds, getting roughly 10 to 12 per cake (for a total of five to six petite layer cakes). Using the correct sprinkles is key so they don't bleed into the cake. I like bright colored confetti sprinkles (surprise!) the best! Also, make no mistake, there are zero eggs in these!

MAKES 5 TO 6 PETITE CAKES

FOR THE CAKE

1½ cups (300 g) granulated sugar

8 tablespoons (113 g) unsalted butter, room temperature, cut into 8 pieces

½ vanilla bean, split and scraped

¾ cup (180 g) sour cream, room temperature

¾ cup (168 g) water, room temperature

½ cup (112 g) sunflower or grapeseed oil

2 tablespoons (28 g) fresh lemon juice (about 1 lemon)

3¼ cups (439 g) all-purpose flour

1½ teaspoons (8 g) baking powder

1 teaspoon (5 g) baking soda

¾ teaspoon sea salt

1 cup (116 g) confetti sprinkles

For the Cake: Preheat the oven to 350°F (177°C). Grease a 9 x 13–inch (23 x 33–cm) baking pan and line with parchment paper, letting the excess hang over the sides. Set aside.

In the bowl of an electric stand mixer fitted with the paddle attachment, add the sugar, butter and vanilla bean seeds (discard the pod) and run on medium until light and fluffy, 4 to 5 minutes.

In a large liquid measuring cup, whisk together the sour cream, water, oil and lemon juice until combined.

In a medium bowl, whisk together the flour, baking powder, baking soda and sea salt. Alternate adding the flour and sour cream mixture in two batches, mixing each addition until combined. Scrape the sides and bottom of the bowl to make sure everything is well combined. Fold the sprinkles into the cake batter and pour the batter into the prepared cake pan, gently tapping the pans on the counter to release any trapped air bubbles and smoothing the top with an offset spatula or the back of a spoon. Make the cake as level as possible so the mini cakes will be easy to stack. Bake in the center of the oven for 50 to 55 minutes. Cool for 20 minutes in the pan before transferring to the rack to cool completely. Once cool, invert the cake onto a cutting board and use a 2½-inch (6-cm) cookie cutter and cut out 10 to 12 cake rounds.

(continued)

FOR THE BUTTERCREAM

5 large egg whites, room temperature

1 cup (200 g) granulated sugar

½ teaspoon cream of tartar

½ teaspoon sea salt

24 tablespoons (339 g) unsalted butter, room temperature, cut into 24 pieces

TO GARNISH

More confetti sprinkles!

For the Buttercream: Add the egg whites and sugar to the clean bowl of an electric stand mixer and nestle it in a saucepan of simmering water over medium-high heat. Do not allow the bottom of the bowl to touch the water. Whisk until the mixture is thick and frothy, the sugar is melted (rub some between two fingers; if it feels gritty, keep whisking) and it's hot to the touch. This should take about 5 minutes. Ideally, you want it to reach 160°F (71°C). Remove the bowl from the heat and transfer it to the stand mixer fitted with the whisk attachment and add the cream of tartar and the salt. Mix on medium-high speed until stiff and glossy and cool to the touch, about 10 minutes (don't rush it). Make sure the meringue is quite stiff and very cool. With the mixer on medium, add in the butter one piece at a time, letting each fully blend before adding in the next. Give it a couple of good stirs with a spatula to knock out any air bubbles.

To Assemble: Place one cake layer on a serving plate and cover with an ample amount of frosting. Place the second layer over the top and cover with the remaining frosting. Dust more confetti sprinkles over the tops and serve.

> **NOTES:** For the buttercream you can add in 1 teaspoon (4 g) of vanilla paste or real vanilla extract (it will darken the color a bit) or about 1 tablespoon (14 g) of fresh lemon juice. Likewise, you can use 2 to 3 teaspoons (4 to 8 g) vanilla extract in the cake base in place of the vanilla bean. Placing the unfrosted cake rounds in the fridge or freezer will make them easier to frost.

CHOCOLATE HAZELNUT PUDDING CAKES
WITH CRÈME ANGLAISE

This dessert is simple, elegant, easy, make-ahead . . . and did I mention gluten free? These are painless to throw together and loaded with chocolate hazelnut flavor. The crème anglaise is equally painless and the perfect mellow counterpoint to these sweet little cakes. The unbaked cakes, crème anglaise and hazelnut crunch can all be made ahead of time and stashed in the fridge. Just pop the cakes in the oven when ready to eat and gently reheat the crème anglaise on the stovetop. The refrigerated unbaked cakes may need an extra minute or two in the oven.

MAKES 4 SERVINGS

FOR THE CRÈME ANGLAISE

½ cup (120 g) whole milk

½ cup (120 g) heavy whipping cream

½ vanilla bean, split and scraped

3 large egg yolks

3 tablespoons (21 g) confectioners' sugar

2 tablespoons (28 g) hazelnut liqueur such as Frangelico®

FOR THE CAKES

8 tablespoons (113 g) unsalted butter, cut into 8 pieces (plus more for the ramekins)

⅔ cup (133 g) granulated sugar, divided

¾ cup (128 g) bittersweet chocolate, finely chopped

3 large eggs, room temperature

⅔ cup (64 g) finely ground hazelnut flour

1 tablespoon (13 g) hazelnut liqueur such as Frangelico® or vanilla paste/real vanilla extract

1 teaspoon (6 g) sea salt

For the Crème Anglaise: Add the milk, cream and vanilla (throw the pod in here, too) to a medium, heavy-bottomed saucepan over medium heat and bring to a simmer.

In a small bowl, whisk together the egg yolks and the confectioners' sugar. Whisk a ladle or two of the warmed milk into the eggs. Once smooth, pour into the saucepan, whisking the whole time. Reduce the heat to medium-low and stir for 3 to 5 minutes more. Don't let it come to a boil. It's ready when it's silky and thickened a bit. It should also coat the back of a spoon and when you run your finger through it, it should leave a track. Whisk in the hazelnut liqueur once off the heat. Use a fine-mesh sieve to strain into a bowl and set aside until ready to use. If making ahead of time, store covered in the fridge and then gently warm before using.

For the Cakes: Preheat the oven to 375°F (191°C). Butter four 8-ounce (226-g) ramekins, sprinkle about 2 teaspoons (8 g) of granulated sugar in the bottom of each ramekin and tap to coat the interior, discarding the excess. Place the ramekins on a baking sheet. Set aside.

Add the chocolate and butter to a medium, heat-safe bowl set over a medium saucepan of simmering water. Do not let the water boil or touch the bowl. Stir frequently until almost smooth. Take off of the heat and continue stirring for about 30 seconds or until completely smooth. Whisk in the eggs, remaining sugar, hazelnut flour, hazelnut liqueur and salt until everything is thoroughly blended. Divide evenly among the prepared ramekins and bake on the baking sheet in the center of the oven for 18 minutes or until the edges are set and the center is jiggly (the middle will look underbaked). Let sit for 8 to 10 minutes, run a knife along the edge and then invert onto a serving plate. The longer they sit the more set the centers will be.

(continued)

CHOCOLATE HAZELNUT PUDDING CAKES
WITH CRÈME ANGLAISE (CONT.)

FOR THE QUICK HAZELNUT CRUNCH

¼ cup (28 g) raw hazelnuts, coarsely chopped

1 tablespoon (14 g) unsalted butter

1 tablespoon (14 g) light brown sugar, packed

¼ teaspoon sea salt

For the Quick Hazelnut Crunch: While the cakes are baking, add the hazelnuts to a small nonstick or cast-iron skillet over medium-low heat and toast for several minutes until lightly bronzed and fragrant. Add the butter, brown sugar and salt and stir until melted and the hazelnuts are evenly coated. Cook for 1 minute more and then transfer to a bowl to cool and set before serving.

To Serve: Pour the crème anglaise over the cakes, sprinkle with the hazelnut crunch and serve immediately.

NOTES: In a pinch you can substitute in almond flour or even all-purpose flour for the hazelnut flour. If using all-purpose flour, fold the flour in last, instead of whisking as the recipe instructs.

While these may seem underbaked, the bake time is enough to cook the eggs to at least 160°F (71°C).

SPICED BROWN SUGAR CAKES

These little cakes (should we call them cupcakes?) are loaded with lots of warm, caramel flavors thanks to the brown sugar and vanilla. This is a swiss meringue buttercream made with brown sugar, instead of the traditional granulated sugar, and then finished with a spiced-up buttercream and sparkling sugar. If you're feeling extra fancy, I highly suggest that you top the cakes with the spiced sparkling sugar for bonus points.

MAKES 13 MINI CAKES

FOR THE CAKES

1 cup (220 g) light brown sugar, packed

3 large eggs, room temperature

½ cup (112 g) sunflower or grapeseed oil

1 cup (125 g) sour cream, room temperature

⅓ cup (75 g) water, room temperature

1 tablespoon (13 g) vanilla paste or real vanilla extract

2 teaspoons (10 g) baking powder

1 teaspoon (5 g) baking soda

1 teaspoon (2 g) cinnamon

½ teaspoon nutmeg

½ teaspoon sea salt

1¾ cups (237 g) all-purpose flour

FOR THE BUTTERCREAM

5 large egg whites, room temperature

1 cup (220 g) light brown sugar, packed

½ teaspoon cream of tartar

½ teaspoon sea salt

24 tablespoons (339 g) unsalted butter, room temperature, cut into 24 pieces

½ vanilla bean, split and scraped, or 2 teaspoons (8 g) vanilla paste or real vanilla extract

½ teaspoon cinnamon

½ teaspoon nutmeg

½ teaspoon ground ginger

¼ teaspoon cardamom

¼ teaspoon cloves

For the Cakes: Preheat the oven to 350°F (177 °C). Grease a regular-sized muffin tin or line with cupcake liners.

In a large bowl, whisk together the sugar and eggs until thick and frothy, about 2 minutes. Slowly stream in the oil, whisking the entire time until it is completely emulsified. If your bowl moves around (I know, you only have two hands), set it on a dish towel to keep it from moving around the counter. Whisk in the sour cream, water, vanilla, baking powder, baking soda, cinnamon, nutmeg and salt. Fold the flour in until just combined; the mixture may be lumpy, which is fine. Scrape the sides and bottom of the bowl to make sure everything is combined. Let the cake batter sit for 30 minutes.

Fill the muffin wells three-fourths full, tap on the counter to release any trapped air bubbles and bake in the center of the oven for 17 to 20 minutes or until when gently pressed in the middle, they bounce back. Let cool for 10 minutes in the tin before turning out onto a rack to finish cooling.

For the Buttercream: Add the egg whites and sugar to the clean bowl of an electric stand mixer and nestle it in a saucepan of simmering water over medium-high heat. Do not allow the bottom of the bowl to touch the water. Whisk until the mixture is thick and frothy, the sugar is melted (rub some between two fingers; if it feels gritty, keep whisking) and it's hot to the touch. This should take about 5 minutes. Ideally you want it to reach 160°F (71°C). Remove the bowl from the heat and transfer it to the stand mixer fitted with the whisk attachment and add the cream of tartar and the salt. Mix on medium-high speed until stiff and glossy and cool to the touch, about 10 minutes (don't rush it). Make sure the meringue is quite stiff and very cool. Make sure the exterior of the bowl is cool to the touch as well. With the mixer on medium, add in the butter one piece at a time, letting each fully blend before adding in the next. Add in the vanilla bean seeds (discard the pod), cinnamon, nutmeg, ginger, cardamom and cloves and run the mixer for 1 minute more or until the spices are evenly distributed throughout. Grab a spatula and give it some aggressive stirs to knock out any air bubbles.

(continued)

SPICED BROWN SUGAR CAKES (CONT.)

FOR THE SPICED SPARKLING SUGAR

½ vanilla bean, split and scraped

½ cup (100 g) sparkling sugar

½ teaspoon cinnamon

½ teaspoon cardamom

½ teaspoon ground ginger

For the Spiced Sparkling Sugar: In a small bowl, massage the vanilla bean seeds (discard the pod) into the sugar. Add in the cinnamon, cardamom and ginger, stirring well to combine.

To Assemble: Smear the buttercream evenly over the tops of the cakes and sprinkle with the spiced sparkling sugar.

> **NOTE:** This makes an ample amount of frosting, so don't be shy adding it to the cakes. If you have any leftover, smear it on graham crackers like my dad does!

KT'S CHOCOLATE CAKES WITH
RASPBERRY CREAM FILLING AND CHOCOLATE GANACHE

My sister requested this recipe, so I'm naming it after her! These are more grocery store cakes from our youth but grown up and made classy, like the superstars they were always destined to be. This is a super-simple chocolate cake base that comes together in a flash and is then loaded up with a raspberry cream center. Topped with a lid of ganache, what could be better?!

MAKES 15 MINI CAKES

FOR THE CAKES

1 cup (200 g) granulated sugar

3 large eggs, room temperature

½ cup (112 g) sunflower or grapeseed oil

½ cup (43 g) unsweetened Dutch-process cocoa powder, sifted

1 tablespoon (14 g) vanilla paste or real vanilla extract

2 teaspoons (10 g) baking powder

1 teaspoon (5 g) baking soda

½ teaspoon sea salt

1 cup (125 g) sour cream, room temperature

1¼ cups (169 g) all-purpose flour

⅓ cup (75 g) hot water

FOR THE CHOCOLATE GANACHE

¾ cup (180 g) heavy whipping cream

¾ cup (128 g) dark chocolate, finely chopped

For the Cakes: Preheat the oven to 350°F (177°C). Grease a regular-sized muffin tin or line with cupcake liners (the cakes will rise more without liners).

In a large bowl, whisk together the sugar and eggs until thick and frothy, about 2 minutes. Slowly stream in the oil, whisking the entire time until it is completely emulsified. If your bowl moves around (I know, you only have two hands), set it on a dish towel to keep it from moving about. Whisk in the cocoa powder, vanilla, baking powder, baking soda and salt. Stir in the sour cream until blended and then fold the flour in until just combined. Pour in the hot water, stirring to combine; be sure to scrape the sides and bottom of the bowl to make sure everything is combined. Let the cake batter sit for 30 minutes.

Fill the muffin wells three-fourths full, tap on the counter to release any trapped air bubbles and bake in the center of the oven for 17 to 20 minutes or until they bounce back when gently pressed in the middle. Let cool for 10 minutes in the tin before turning out onto a rack to finish cooling completely.

For the Chocolate Ganache: Add the cream and chocolate to a medium, heat-safe bowl set over a medium saucepan of simmering water. Do not let the water boil or touch the bowl. Stir frequently until almost smooth. Take off of the heat and stir periodically while you make the raspberry cream. When ready, the ganache should be thick but pourable.

(continued)

FOR THE RASPBERRY CREAM

2 large egg whites, room temperature

½ cup (100 g) granulated sugar

1 tablespoon (21 g) light corn syrup

½ teaspoon cream of tartar

½ teaspoon sea salt

⅓ cup (107 g) raspberry jam

For the Raspberry Cream: Add the egg whites, sugar and corn syrup to the clean bowl of an electric stand mixer and nestle it in a saucepan of simmering water over medium-high heat. Do not allow the bottom of the bowl to touch the water. Whisk until the mixture is thick and frothy, the sugar is melted (rub some between two fingers; if it feels gritty, keep whisking) and it's hot to the touch. This should take about 5 minutes. Ideally, you want it to reach 160°F (71°C). Remove the bowl from the heat, transfer it to the stand mixer fitted with the whisk attachment and add the cream of tartar and salt. Mix on medium-high speed until stiff and glossy and cool to the touch, about 10 minutes (don't rush it). Take the bowl out of the mixer and fold in the raspberry jam. Fit one pastry bag with a medium round tip and the other with a small French star tip (I used Ateco 804 and 862 respectively). Put two-thirds of the raspberry cream in the bag fitted with the round tip and the remaining in the bag with the French star tip.

To Assemble: Gently remove some of the cake from the center of the cupcakes (you can use a small spoon, knife or an apple corer). Use the pastry bag fitted with the round tip to fill the cake centers with the raspberry cream. Fill them all the way up to the top so that the top surface is smooth. Spoon the ganache over the tops. Let set for 30 minutes or so and then, using the bag fitted with the French star, pipe over the top of the cakes.

NOTE: Feel free to use any fruit jam for these!

"There'll be parties for hosting,
marshmallows for toasting
and caroling out in the snow."

—Andy Williams

HOLIDAY **CAKES**
The Most Wonderful Time of the Year

Really, it is! My favorite season for baking, for socializing, for martinis and cake. My favorite holiday cakes are a little bit classic and a little bit jazz-handsy. Because I know how crazy this time of year is, most of these cakes are pretty effortless or have lots of make-ahead components.

So, what I first want you to do is put on some soft clothes and turn on some holiday music. Maybe light a candle if you're feeling it. Pour yourself some spiked eggnog? I'm just throwing around ideas for you. The point being, baking should be relaxing and fun, so create a vibe that makes you relaxed and happy.

Now, pick any one of these holiday favorites and have a go at it. If I was pressed for time and needed something festive, I would probably reach for the Spiced Vanilla Crème Caramel (page 173), which can be made quickly days in advance of serving and has a mega wow factor when the pan is inverted and the caramel puddles on top of the custard.

If I really wanted to dazzle with minimal effort, I would throw together the Wintery Pavlova with Port Cranberries and Rosemary (page 170) the morning of my get-together. Let the pavlova sit in the turned-off oven all day, leave your cranberries on the counter in a lidded container and all you have to do prior to serving is whip up some cream to serve it with. This one screams holiday to me.

When I have a holiday baking project in mind, I reach for one of the layer cakes, such as the Muscovado Gingerbread Cake with Salted Caramel Buttercream (page 174) or the Chocolate Peppermint Bûche de Noël (page 180), which is a heap of fun to throw together.

Wishing that this holiday season is your best one ever!

WINTERY PAVLOVA WITH
PORT CRANBERRIES AND ROSEMARY

Everybody needs a good pavlova recipe in their back pocket. I love that you can make one the day before serving and let it sit in the oven overnight to stay nice and crisp on the exterior and marshmallow-heaven in the center. This is topped with an ample cloud of not-too-sweet whipped cream and my favorite holiday cranberries.

MAKES 8 TO 10 SERVINGS

FOR THE PAVLOVA

5 large egg whites

1 cup (200 g) granulated sugar

1 teaspoon (3 g) cream of tartar

½ teaspoon sea salt

¼ cup (30 g) confectioners' sugar

1 teaspoon (4 g) vanilla paste or real vanilla extract

FOR THE CRANBERRIES

½ cup (112 g) water

⅓ cup (73 g) light brown sugar, packed

⅓ cup (75 g) Ruby Port

6 ounces (170 g) fresh or frozen cranberries

½ cup (64 g) dried tart cherries

1 sprig rosemary

1 tablespoon (15 g) red wine vinegar

1 teaspoon (2 g) five-spice powder

FOR THE WHIPPED CREAM

1½ cups (360 g) heavy whipping cream, cold

4½ tablespoons (32 g) confectioners' sugar

NOTE: If you live in an area with high humidity, your pavlova should be made the same day it is served and may need more time in the oven to achieve a crispy exterior.

For the Pavlova: Preheat the oven to 350°F (177°C). Line a baking sheet with parchment paper.

Add the egg whites and sugar to the clean bowl of an electric stand mixer and nestle it in a saucepan of simmering water over medium-high heat. Do not allow the bottom of the bowl to touch the water. Whisk until the mixture is thick and frothy, the sugar is melted (rub some between two fingers; if it feels gritty, keep whisking) and it's hot to the touch. This should take about 5 minutes. Ideally you want it to reach 160°F (71°C). Remove the bowl from the heat, transfer it to the stand mixer fitted with the whisk attachment and add the cream of tartar and salt. Mix on medium-high speed until stiff and glossy and cool to the touch, about 10 minutes (don't rush it). Add the confectioners' sugar and vanilla and run the machine for 1 minute more. Make a mound of meringue on the prepared baking sheet 8 to 9 inches (20 to 23 cm) in circumference. Use the back of a spoon to create a slight valley in the middle to hold all of the toppings post-bake.

Place in the center of the oven, immediately reduce the temperature to 200°F (93°C) and bake for 2 hours. Check midway through the bake time to make sure it's not browning and still white. If it's taking on any color, turn the oven down to 180°F (82° C). Once done, let the meringue cool completely inside the turned-off oven. When done, it should be crispy on the exterior and marshmallow-delicious in the interior. It should take several hours to cool down and be the proper consistency. Leave in the turned-off oven until ready to serve.

For the Cranberries: In a medium, heavy-bottomed saucepan, add the water, brown sugar and port over medium heat, stirring until the sugar is melted. Add in the cranberries, cherries, rosemary, vinegar and five-spice powder and simmer for 15 to 20 minutes until the liquid has reduced and most of the cranberries are still plump (it's okay if some have popped). Pour into a heat-safe bowl to cool completely. Remove the rosemary sprig before using.

For the Whipped Cream: Place the cold heavy whipping cream in the bowl of an electric stand mixer fitted with the whisk attachment. Whisk on medium until soft peaks form. Sprinkle the confectioners' sugar over the top and whisk until soft peaks return, taking care not to overbeat the cream.

To Assemble: Place the pavlova on a serving plate and pile high with the whipped cream. Put the cranberries on top just prior to serving.

SPICED VANILLA CRÈME CARAMEL

This is one of those fabulous desserts that looks complicated but isn't in the slightest. You whip up a quick caramel and cover the bottom of a cake pan with it. On top of this you bake up a luscious custard, scented with holiday spices and vanilla. Crème caramels need to chill for at least 12 hours or up to several days. This chill time lets the caramel soften so that when you invert the custard onto a rimmed serving plate, you'll get a cascade of caramel. This one's a beauty and the ultimate make-ahead dessert!

MAKES 8 TO 10 SERVINGS

FOR THE CARAMEL
¾ cup (150 g) granulated sugar

FOR THE SPICED-VANILLA CUSTARD
1½ cups (360 g) whole milk

1 cup (240 g) heavy whipping cream

¾ cup (150 g) granulated sugar

½ vanilla bean, split and scraped, or 2 teaspoons (8 g) vanilla paste/real vanilla extract

¼ teaspoon cinnamon

¼ teaspoon nutmeg

3 large eggs

3 large egg yolks

Preheat the oven to 325°F (163°C).

For the Caramel: Place the sugar in a small, heavy-bottomed saucepan and cook over medium-high heat until the sugar melts and turns a beautiful caramel color, 5 minutes; stir periodically. Don't let it get too hot and burn. Once it's caramel colored, pour it into an ungreased, 8-inch (20-cm) round cake pan, turning the pan to coat the bottom quickly and completely; it will harden up fast. Set the pan inside a larger roasting pan. Let cool completely. Boil some water; set aside.

For the Spiced-Vanilla Custard: In a large, heavy-bottomed saucepan set over medium heat, add the milk, cream, sugar, vanilla bean seeds and pod, cinnamon and nutmeg and simmer until the milk is warm and the sugar is dissolved, about 5 minutes. Discard the pod and let cool for 5 minutes.

In a medium bowl, whisk together the eggs and egg yolks and then whisk the milk mixture slowly into the eggs, constantly whisking so as not to scramble the eggs. Strain the mixture through a fine-mesh sieve into the pan with the caramel. Pour the hot water into the roasting pan, taking care not to get any in with the custard and only filling halfway up the side of the pan. Cover the cake pan in foil and carefully transfer to the middle of the oven and bake for 45 to 50 minutes. The center will still be jiggly; that's good! Remove the custard pan from the water bath (careful!) and set on a rack to cool for about 1 hour and then wrap tightly and refrigerate overnight or at least 12 hours.

To Serve: Run a knife around the outer edge of the custard and invert the custard onto a rimmed serving plate. Serve immediately.

MUSCOVADO GINGERBREAD CAKE
WITH SALTED CARAMEL BUTTERCREAM

Oh muscovado, how I love thee! Muscovado is an unprocessed brown sugar that has heaps of caramel notes and pairs beautifully with the flavors of the holiday (think molasses, five-spice, cranberries and pumpkin). This is a gorgeously damp, heavily gingered cake with mounds of salted caramel buttercream. Both the cake and the caramel can be made ahead of time; you need only whip up the buttercream and assemble on the day of your celebration. This cake has a lot of ingredients!!! Most are spices and zest, so don't be put off. Trust me, she's worth it!

MAKES 10 TO 12 SERVINGS

FOR THE CARAMEL

½ cup (110 g) dark brown sugar, packed

6 tablespoons (85 g) unsalted butter

¼ cup (60 g) heavy whipping cream, room temperature

½ teaspoon sea salt

1 teaspoon (4 g) vanilla paste or real vanilla extract

FOR THE CAKE

¾ cup (165 g) dark muscovado sugar, packed

¼ cup (50 g) granulated sugar

1½ tablespoons (9 g) ground ginger

1 tablespoon (6 g) fresh ginger, finely minced or grated

1 tablespoon (2 g) orange zest (about 1 orange)

1 tablespoon (6 g) cinnamon

1 teaspoon (2 g) cloves

1 teaspoon (2 g) nutmeg

1 teaspoon (2 g) allspice

¾ teaspoon cardamom

8 tablespoons (113 g) unsalted butter, softened

3 large eggs, room temperature

¾ cup (168 g) sunflower or grapeseed oil

1 cup (336 g) unsulphured molasses (not blackstrap)

1 tablespoon (13 g) vanilla paste or real vanilla extract

For the Caramel: Add the brown sugar and butter to a medium, heavy-bottomed saucepan over medium heat and whisk until the sugar is dissolved and turns a rich, deep caramel color. Slowly pour in the heavy cream, turn up the heat to medium-high and continue whisking until it reaches a boil. Reduce to medium heat for about 5 minutes or until thickened. Stir in the salt and vanilla and set aside to cool, whisking periodically. If it starts to separate, whisk until completely blended once again. Chill in the fridge a bit and then bring closer to room temperature before using; this will allow it to become the correct consistency for the buttercream.

For the Cake: Preheat the oven to 350°F (177°C). Grease two 8-inch (20-cm) round cake pans and line with parchment paper.

In the bowl of an electric stand mixer fitted with the paddle attachment, add the muscovado sugar, granulated sugar, ground ginger, fresh ginger, orange zest, cinnamon, cloves, nutmeg, allspice and cardamom and run the mixer on low to combine. You can get in there and massage the ginger, spices and zest into the sugar if you're feeling it. Add the butter and run the mixer on medium for 4 to 5 minutes or until light and fluffy (the muscovado won't make it as light as if it was just regular sugar, but it should have some fluff to it). With the mixer on low, add in the eggs, one at a time, making sure that each is well blended before adding the next. Periodically scrape the sides and bottom of the bowl to make sure everything is incorporated. With the mixer on low, stream in the oil and then the molasses and vanilla. Take the bowl out of the mixer and set aside.

In a medium bowl whisk together the flour, baking soda and salt. Alternate adding the flour and the buttermilk to the sugar mixture in two batches, mixing each until combined. Divide evenly between the prepared pans, tapping on the counter to release any trapped air bubbles and smoothing the tops with an offset spatula or the back of a spoon. Bake in the center of the oven for 45 minutes or until puffed and the center bounces back when gently pressed. Set the pans on a cooling rack. After 10 minutes, run a knife around the edges and turn the cakes out onto the rack to cool completely. Discard the parchment.

(continued)

MUSCOVADO GINGERBREAD CAKE
WITH SALTED CARAMEL BUTTERCREAM (CONT.)

3¼ cups (439 g) all-purpose flour

2 teaspoons (10 g) baking soda

1 teaspoon (6 g) sea salt

1 cup (240 g) buttermilk, shaken and room temperature

FOR THE SALTED CARAMEL BUTTERCREAM

5 large egg whites

1 cup (200 g) granulated sugar

½ teaspoon cream of tartar

½ teaspoon sea salt

24 tablespoons (339 g) unsalted butter, room temperature, cut into 24 pieces

⅓ cup (89 g) caramel (recipe above)

For the Salted Caramel Buttercream: Add the egg whites and sugar to the clean bowl of an electric stand mixer and nestle it in a saucepan of simmering water over medium-high heat. Do not allow the bottom of the bowl to touch the water. Whisk until the mixture is thick and frothy, the sugar is melted (rub some between two fingers; if it feels gritty, keep whisking) and it's hot to the touch. This should take about 5 minutes. Ideally, you want it to reach 160°F (71°C). Remove the bowl from the heat and transfer it to the stand mixer fitted with the whisk attachment and add the cream of tartar and the salt. Mix on medium-high speed until stiff and glossy and cool to the touch, about 10 minutes (don't rush it). Make sure the meringue is quite stiff and very cool. Make sure the bowl is cool to the touch as well (you can stash in the fridge for 5 minutes to help cool it down). With the mixer on medium add in the butter one piece at a time, letting each fully blend before adding in the next. Take the bowl out of the mixer and fold in the caramel until you still see streaks of caramel throughout, and it's not completely blended.

To Assemble: Place one cake layer upside down on a cake plate and cover with an ample amount of frosting. Place the second layer over the top, right side up, and cover with the remaining frosting. Use an offset spatula or the back of a spoon to make all of the swoops and swirls. Serve with the remaining caramel on the side.

> **NOTE:** In a pinch, you can sub in brown sugar, ideally dark brown sugar, for the muscovado.

DULCE DE LECHE PUMPKIN CHEESECAKE

Every year I make a pumpkin cheesecake with caramel for our Thanksgiving table. This is inspired by one of my favorites from DisplacedHousewife.com and you are going to LOVE it! It can be made days ahead of time, which is probably what makes it one of my favorite holiday desserts (aside from it tasting delicious!). At a minimum, the cheesecake needs 12 hours in the fridge to set and chill. The three best tips for success with this cheesecake: try to get rid of excess moisture in the pumpkin puree; have EVERYTHING at room temperature; mix everything low and slow; and avoid sudden temperature changes. All of this should yield a beautiful, crack-free cheesecake! See more tips in the headnote for the Boozy Strawberry-Basil Cheesecake (page 25).

MAKES 10 TO 12 SERVINGS

TO START
15 ounces (1¾ cups [425 g]) 100% pure pureed pumpkin (not pie filling)

FOR THE CRUST
12 whole graham crackers (6 oz [180 g])

3 tablespoons (42 g) light brown sugar, packed

5 tablespoons (70 g) unsalted butter, melted

FOR THE PUMPKIN CHEESECAKE
14 ounces (398 g) cream cheese, room temperature

1½ cups (330 g) light brown sugar, packed

½ teaspoon cinnamon

¼ teaspoon cloves

¼ teaspoon ground ginger

¼ teaspoon nutmeg

1 teaspoon (6 g) sea salt

4 large eggs, room temperature

8 ounces (240 g) sour cream, room temperature

1 tablespoon (14 g) fresh orange juice

2 teaspoons (8 g) vanilla paste or real vanilla extract

To Start: Spread the pumpkin puree on a couple of layers of paper or cloth towels to release any excess moisture. You may need to replace the towels several times if the pumpkin is quite moist. Let sit out and dry until ready to add to the cheesecake.

For the Crust: Preheat the oven to 350°F (177°C). Grease a 9-inch (23-cm) nonstick springform pan and line with parchment paper.

Put the graham crackers and brown sugar in a food processor or high-speed blender and pulse until the mixture becomes a very fine crumb. Drizzle the butter on top and pulse until just mixed and it resembles wet sand. Firmly and evenly press the mixture into the bottom of the springform. Place the crust in the oven for 10 to 12 minutes or until it starts to turn a little golden and is bronzed around the edges. Set the crust aside to cool completely.

For the Pumpkin Cheesecake: Increase the oven temperature to 400°F (200°C) and place a heat-safe skillet or Dutch oven on the bottom rack. Bring 4 cups (1 L) of water to a boil and set aside while you prepare the cheesecake.

In the bowl of an electric stand mixer fitted with the paddle attachment, mix the cream cheese, sugar, cinnamon, cloves, ginger, nutmeg and salt on low for about 2 minutes or until smooth and lump free. Frequently use a spatula to scrape down the sides and bottom of the bowl to make sure everything is incorporated.

In a small bowl, lightly whisk the eggs and then slowly stream them into the bowl with the mixer on low. Continue with the mixer on low for 2 minutes or until combined. Add in the pumpkin, sour cream, orange juice and vanilla, making sure each addition is well blended before adding in the next; mix on low for another 2 minutes or until well blended. Use the back of your spatula to smash down any rogue chunks of cream cheese. Press the mixture through a fine-mesh sieve into the cooled crust, smoothing the top with an offset spatula or the back of a spoon.

(continued)

DULCE DE LECHE PUMPKIN CHEESECAKE (CONT.)

FOR THE DULCE DE LECHE

1 cup (240 g) whole milk

1 cup (240 g) heavy whipping cream

⅔ cup (150 g) granulated sugar

½ vanilla bean, split and scraped, or 2 teaspoons (8 g) vanilla paste or real vanilla extract

½ teaspoon sea salt

½ teaspoon baking soda

Place the cheesecake in the center of the oven and pour the hot water into the skillet on the bottom rack and quickly shut the oven door. Bake the cheesecake for 15 minutes and then reduce the oven to 250°F (121°C) and bake for an additional 45 minutes. When done, the center will jiggle when gently shaken and the edges will be set. Turn off the oven and let the cheesecake sit in it for 30 minutes, with the door open. After 30 minutes, take the cheesecake out of the oven. Let it sit at room temperature for about 1 hour. When cool, wrap tightly in plastic wrap (still in the springform pan) and set in the fridge to chill overnight.

For the Dulce de Leche: In a large, heavy-bottomed saucepan set over high heat, whisk together the milk, cream, sugar, vanilla bean seeds and pod and salt and bring to a boil. Reduce to a simmer and whisk in the baking soda. Whenever you walk by the pot, give it a stir and adjust the temperature to keep it from boiling; you just want some bubbles around the edges of the pan. Usually between the 30- to 45-minute mark, the color starts to deepen, and the mixture begins to thicken a bit. When this happens, it's going to be more prone to a heavy boil (which you don't want), so stick near it, adjusting the temperature as necessary and stirring more frequently. It should be done at around 1½ to 2 hours. You want the dulce to have reduced and thickened as well as become bronzed with a deep caramel color. Strain the dulce into a heat-safe, lidded container and stash in the fridge until ready to use. It will thicken more as it cools. Let it come closer to room temperature before using.

To Assemble: Gently run a knife around the edge of the cheesecake, remove the cheesecake from the pan and set on a cake plate. Pour the dulce over the top of the cheesecake and serve.

CHOCOLATE PEPPERMINT BÛCHE DE NOËL

Yule logs are not hard to make; in fact, they come together quite quickly. I highly recommend reading through the instructions first (really!) and you'll be surprised at how easy it is. The styling for this cake was totally inspired by a cake that John Whaite posted on social media several years back. I was captivated by the holiday vibes but also the simplicity. Play around with the meringue until you get it looking just right. Using a kitchen torch also lets you get the perfect char on your faux log.

When Gavin was in middle school, he volunteered us to make a bûche de noël for an event at his school . . . for the entire school. This is the recipe I created and I love it. We ended up making six or seven that day. I'm still waiting for my mom-of-the-year award, if anyone happens to know when it might arrive.

MAKES 10 TO 12 SERVINGS

FOR THE CAKE

5 large eggs, separated

⅔ cup (133 g) granulated sugar, divided

4 tablespoons (57 g) unsalted butter, melted and cooled

2 tablespoons (30 g) whole milk, room temperature

2 teaspoons (8 g) vanilla paste or real vanilla extract

⅔ cup (90 g) all-purpose flour

¼ cup (21 g) unsweetened Dutch-process cocoa powder, sifted

¾ teaspoon baking powder

½ teaspoon baking soda

½ teaspoon sea salt

For the Cake: Preheat the oven to 350°F (177°C). Grease a 16 x 11–inch (41 x 28–cm) rimmed baking sheet and cover with a layer of parchment paper. Grease the parchment paper as well. Cut another piece of parchment that's the same size and set aside.

In the bowl of an electric stand mixer fitted with the whisk attachment, add the egg yolks (set the whites aside for the next step), ⅓ cup (67 g) of sugar, melted butter, milk and vanilla and whisk on medium until light and smooth, about 3 minutes. Transfer to a large bowl and set aside. Thoroughly clean and dry the whisk attachment and mixing bowl.

In the bowl of an electric stand mixer fitted with the whisk attachment, add the egg whites and whisk on medium for 1 to 2 minutes or until frothy and opaque. With the mixer on low, slowly stream in the remaining ⅓ cup (67 g) of sugar over the course of 1 minute. Turn the mixer up to high and whisk for about 1 minute more or until they hold medium peaks; do not overmix.

In a small bowl, whisk together the flour, cocoa powder, baking powder, baking soda and salt. Add to the egg yolk mixture and mix well. Fold in the egg whites in three batches, taking care not to deflate them but also making sure that there are no hidden lumps of meringue. Spread the mixture in an even layer, ¼ to ½ inch (6 mm to 1.3 cm) thick, in the shape of a rectangle (doesn't have to be perfect) onto the prepared baking sheet. Bake in the center of the oven for 12 to 14 minutes.

Dust the extra piece of parchment paper evenly with cocoa powder. As soon as the cake gets out of the oven, flip the cake onto the cocoa-covered parchment paper. Peel the older layer of parchment off of the backside of the cake. Carefully roll the cake up, jelly roll–style and let cool.

(continued)

FOR THE WHITE CHOCOLATE-PEPPERMINT BUTTERCREAM FILLING

8 tablespoons (113 g) unsalted butter, room temperature, cut into 8 pieces

1½ cups (180 g) confectioners' sugar, sifted

1 cup (170 g) good-quality white chocolate, melted and cooled

2 tablespoons (30 g) heavy whipping cream, room temperature

1½ teaspoons (6 g) peppermint extract

¼ teaspoon sea salt

⅓ cup (53 g) peppermint candy, finely crushed

FOR THE MERINGUE

3 large egg whites

¾ cup (150 g) granulated sugar

2 tablespoons (42 g) light corn syrup

¼ teaspoon cream of tartar

¼ teaspoon sea salt

½ teaspoon vanilla paste or real vanilla extract

TO GARNISH

Fresh rosemary sprigs

Confectioners' sugar

Cocoa powder

Gold/silver sprinkles

For the White Chocolate–Peppermint Buttercream Filling: In the bowl of an electric stand mixer fitted with the paddle attachment, add the butter and sugar and mix on medium until smooth and completely combined. With the mixer on low, stream in the cooled white chocolate. Add in the heavy whipping cream, peppermint extract and salt and mix on medium for 1 minute. Take the bowl out of the mixer and fold in the crushed peppermint candy.

For the Meringue: Add the egg whites, sugar and corn syrup to the clean bowl of an electric stand mixer and nestle it in a saucepan of simmering water over medium-high heat. Do not allow the bottom of the bowl to touch the water. Whisk until the mixture is opaque and frothy, the sugar is melted (rub some between two fingers; if it feels gritty, keep whisking) and it's warm to the touch. Remove the bowl from the heat, transfer it to the stand mixer fitted with the whisk attachment and add the cream of tartar and salt. Mix on medium-high speed until stiff and glossy and cool to the touch, 3 to 5 minutes. Add in the vanilla and mix for 20 seconds more.

To Assemble: Gently unroll the cake and, in an even layer, frost with the white chocolate–peppermint buttercream. Carefully roll the cake back up, discarding the parchment paper. Place the cake roll seam side down on a flat serving plate. Cut off the ends to reveal a nice, clean swirl of cake and buttercream. Cover the outside of the cake with the meringue using an offset spatula. Make long strokes along the length of the cake to give the texture and look of a log and make a circular pattern on the ends. Use a torch, in a circular motion, to make some nice "log" burn marks.

To Garnish: Place some sprigs of rosemary on top (you can dust with confectioners' sugar for a snow effect). You can also dust with cocoa powder over the meringue to emphasize the log vibes, add sprinkles, whatever feels fun! Serve immediately.

SPICED EGGNOG CAKE
WITH RUM BUTTERCREAM

Raise your hand if you're a member of the eggnog appreciation club! My love of eggnog runs deep, and I love turning it into cheesecake, cookies, pies, custards . . . you name it. So, it's surprising to no one that we have an eggnog cake before us right now. This cake is 25 shades of heaven. Light and fluffy, perfectly spiced and boozy . . . it deserves a standing spot on your holiday dessert table!

MAKES 8 TO 10 SERVINGS

FOR THE CAKE

1 cup (220 g) light brown sugar, packed

1 cup (200 g) granulated sugar

8 tablespoons (113 g) unsalted butter, room temperature, cut into 8 pieces

1½ teaspoons (3 g) nutmeg

1 teaspoon (2 g) cinnamon

3 large eggs, room temperature

½ cup (112 g) sunflower or grapeseed oil

1 tablespoon (13 g) vanilla paste or real vanilla extract

1 teaspoon (4 g) rum extract

3 cups, plus 3 tablespoons (432 g) all-purpose flour

1 teaspoon (5 g) baking powder

1 teaspoon (5 g) baking soda

1 teaspoon (6 g) sea salt

1 cup (240 g) whole milk, room temperature

¾ cup (180 g) sour cream, room temperature

For the Cake: Preheat the oven to 350°F (177°C). Grease two 8-inch (20-cm) round cake pans and line with parchment paper.

In the bowl of an electric stand mixer fitted with the paddle attachment, add the brown sugar, granulated sugar, butter, nutmeg and cinnamon and mix on medium for 4 to 5 minutes or until light and fluffy. Add in the eggs, one at a time, making sure each is well blended before adding in the next. Periodically scrape the sides and bottom of the bowl so that everything is well blended. With the mixer on low, stream in the oil. Add in the vanilla and rum extract and mix for about 1 minute more or until combined.

In a medium bowl, whisk together the flour, baking powder, baking soda and salt. In a large, liquid measuring cup whisk together the milk and sour cream. Alternate adding the flour and milk to the butter mixture in two batches, mixing each until just combined. Divide evenly between the prepared pans, tapping on the counter to release any trapped air bubbles and smoothing the tops with an offset spatula or the back of a spoon. Bake in the center of the oven for 40 to 45 minutes or until puffed and the center bounces back when gently pressed. Set the pans on a cooling rack. After ten minutes, run a knife around the edges and turn the cakes out onto the rack to cool completely.

(continued)

FOR THE SPICED RUM SOAK
½ cup (100 g) granulated sugar

¼ cup (56 g) boiling water

¼ cup (56 g) good-quality rum

½ teaspoon nutmeg

FOR THE SPICED FRENCH BUTTERCREAM
1 cup (200 g) granulated sugar

⅔ cup (150 g) water, room temperature

8 large egg yolks

24 tablespoons (344 g) unsalted butter, room temperature, cut into 24 pieces

2 teaspoons (8 g) rum extract

2 teaspoons (4 g) vanilla paste or real vanilla extract

1 teaspoon (2 g) nutmeg

TO GARNISH
Fresh grated nutmeg

For the Spiced Rum Soak: Combine the sugar and water in a small bowl and whisk until the sugar is completely dissolved. Whisk in the rum and nutmeg and set aside to cool. Once the soak and the cakes are cool, brush the soak over the top of the cakes, allowing time for it to absorb.

For the Spiced French Buttercream: Add the sugar and water to a medium, heavy-bottomed saucepan over medium-low heat and cook for 20 minutes or until it reaches 240°F (116°C). The sugar will be completely dissolved, but it should not have changed color. Keep an eye on it so that it doesn't start to darken. Don't stir as you don't want to splash the liquid up the sides of the pan.

When the sugar water is almost ready, add the egg yolks to the bowl of an electric stand mixer fitted with the whisk attachment and whisk on high for 4 minutes, or until they have lightened in color. When the sugar is ready, turn the mixer on medium-low and slowly stream the screaming-hot sugar water in toward the side of the bowl; be careful not to hit the whisk. Once all of the sugar is added, turn the mixer on high and whisk until the bottom of the bowl feels cool. Once cool, turn the mixer down to medium and add in the butter, one chunk at a time, making sure it is completely blended before adding in the next chunk. Add in the rum extract, vanilla and nutmeg and run the mixer for 30 seconds more. Remove the bowl from the mixer and give it a couple of good stirs with a spatula to get rid of any air bubbles.

To Assemble: Place one cake layer upside-down on a cake plate and cover with an ample amount of buttercream. Place the second layer over the top, right side up, and cover with the remaining buttercream. Use an offset spatula or the back of a spoon to make all of the swoops and swirls. Finish with a dusting of fresh grated nutmeg.

> **NOTE:** Rum extract can be found in the baking aisle near the vanilla extract.

ACKNOWLEDGMENTS

I'd first and foremost like to thank Stella and Gavin! This has been a weird year, to say the least, and you have handled it (and me being consumed with writing this book) like the true ballers you are. I love you!

I'd like to thank everyone from Page Street that worked on *The Cake Book*, especially Marissa Giambelluca and Meg Baskis. This is our second time around, and I couldn't be happier to be paired with you or prouder and more excited with this book! I have truly enjoyed every minute of this journey.

Liz Parker, you're a dream! There when I need you, getting things done. I so appreciate you.

To all of my cake testers—Hilary, Natalie, Mom, Mike, Christie, Kelly, Stella—a big, heartfelt thank you!!! Your feedback and time were invaluable in making *The Cake Book*.

I'd like to thank Smith and Saint, specifically Kaila and Britt. You both made it possible to keep the lights on at DisplacedHousewife.com while I worked on this book. You kept me on point, on time, with wonderful projects, and I'm so grateful for your management!

My work friends, all over the globe, that are all equally obsessed with food and books as much as I am. This includes Kevin, Brian, Adam, Ryan, Christine, Jessie, Amanda, Kylie, Amisha and Aliza. Thank you for your conversation, encouragement and helpful feedback on this cake journey—I love you all so much!

Susan Clark at Sweetheart Ceramics—your work inspires me so much!!

To all of the amazing cake women and bakers before me, thanks for paving the way with your hard work and creativity.

And last, but definitely not least, to all of the people that follow and bake from DisplacedHousewife.com and *The Cookie Book*, THANK YOU. I love this community, I love your emails and questions, I love your DMs, your sense of humor, your insight and seeing photos of what you baked up. You making the recipes I've created, sharing them with friends and family, using them to mark special occasions is what this is all about. I'm honored to be a part of your lives, truly.

xox

ABOUT THE AUTHOR

Rebecca Firth is a food writer, photographer, creator of the sweets-focused blog DisplacedHousewife.com and author of the best-selling cookbook *The Cookie Book*. Rebecca was a finalist of the 2017 Saveur Blog Award (Baking & Sweets category) and her work has appeared in *Bake from Scratch*, Tasting Table, *Sunset* magazine, BuzzFeed, *Food & Wine*, *Teen Vogue* and the *Washington Post*. *The Cake Book* is her second cookbook. She lives with her family in the Santa Ynez Valley, California.

INDEX